W9-CER-121

"Congress shall make no law . . . abridging the freedom of speech, or of the press."

First Amendment to the U.S. Constitution

The basic foundation of our democracy is the first amendment guarantee of freedom of expression. The Opposing Viewpoints Series is dedicated to the concept of this basic freedom and the idea that it is more important to practice it than to enshrine it.

Contents

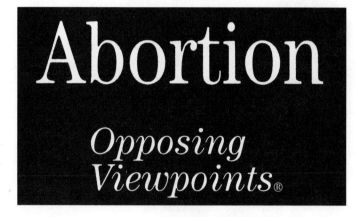

Abortion

Opposing Viewpoints®

Other Books of Related Interest in the Opposing Viewpoints Series:

Why Consider Opposing Viewpoints?

"It is better to debate a question without settling it than to settle a question without debating it."

Joseph Joubert (1754-1824)

The Importance of Examining Opposing Viewpoints

The purpose of the Opposing Viewpoints Series, and this book in particular, is to present balanced, and often difficult to find, opposing points of view on complex and sensitive issues.

Probably the best way to become informed is to analyze the positions of those who are regarded as experts and well studied on issues. It is important to consider every variety of opinion in an attempt to determine the truth. Opinions from the mainstream of society should be examined. But also important are opinions that are considered radical, reactionary, or minority as well as those stigmatized by some other uncomplimentary label. An important lesson of history is the eventual acceptance of many unpopular and even despised opinions. The ideas of Socrates, Jesus, and Galileo are good examples of this.

Readers will approach this book with their own opinions on the issues debated within it. However, to have a good grasp of one's own viewpoint, it is necessary to understand the arguments of those with whom one disagrees. It can be said that those who do not completely understand their adversary's point of view do not fully understand their own.

A persuasive case for considering opposing viewpoints has been presented by John Stuart Mill in his work *On Liberty*. When examining controversial issues it may be helpful to reflect on this suggestion:

The only way in which a human being can make some approach to knowing the whole of a subject, is by hearing what can be said about it by persons of every variety of opinion, and studying all modes in which it can be looked at by every character of mind. No wise man ever acquired his wisdom in any mode but this.

Analyzing Sources of Information

The Opposing Viewpoints Series includes diverse materials taken from magazines, journals, books, and newspapers, as well as statements and position papers from a wide range of individuals, organizations, and governments. This broad spectrum of sources helps to develop patterns of thinking which are open to the consideration of a variety of opinions.

Pitfalls to Avoid

A pitfall to avoid in considering opposing points of view is that of regarding one's own opinion as being common sense and the most rational stance, and the point of view of others as being only opinion and naturally wrong. It may be that another's opinion is correct and one's own is in error.

Another pitfall to avoid is that of closing one's mind to the opinions of those with whom one disagrees. The best way to approach a dialogue is to make one's primary purpose that of understanding the mind and arguments of the other person and not that of enlightening him or her with one's own solutions. More can be learned by listening than speaking.

It is my hope that after reading this book the reader will have a deeper understanding of the issues debated and will appreciate the complexity of even seemingly simple issues on which good and honest people disagree. This awareness is particularly important in a democratic society such as ours where people enter into public debate to determine the common good. Those with whom one disagrees should not necessarily be regarded as enemies, but perhaps simply as people who suggest different paths to a common goal.

Developing Basic Reading and Thinking Skills

In this book, carefully edited opposing viewpoints are purposely placed back to back to create a running debate; each viewpoint is preceded by a short quotation that best expresses the author's main argument. This format instantly plunges the reader into the midst of a controversial issue and greatly aids that reader in mastering the basic skill of recognizing an author's point of view.

A number of basic skills for critical thinking are practiced in the activities that appear throughout the books in the series. Some of the skills are:

Evaluating Sources of Information. The ability to choose from among alternative sources the most reliable and accurate source in relation to a given subject.

Separating Fact from Opinion. The ability to make the basic distinction between factual statements (those that can be demonstrated or verified empirically) and statements of opinion (those that are beliefs or attitudes that cannot be proved).

Identifying Stereotypes. The ability to identify oversimplified, exaggerated descriptions (favorable or unfavorable) about people and insulting statements about racial, religious, or national groups, based upon misinformation or lack of information.

Recognizing Ethnocentrism. The ability to recognize attitudes or opinions that express the view that one's own race, culture, or group is inherently superior, or those attitudes that judge another culture or group in terms of one's own.

It is important to consider opposing viewpoints and equally important to be able to critically analyze those viewpoints. The activities in this book are designed to help the reader master these thinking skills. Statements are taken from the book's viewpoints and the reader is asked to analyze them. This technique aids the reader in developing skills that not only can be applied to the viewpoints in this book, but also to situations where opinionated spokespersons comment on controversial issues. Although the activities are helpful to the solitary reader, they are most useful when the reader can benefit from the interaction of group discussion.

Using this book and others in the series should help readers develop basic reading and thinking skills. These skills should improve the reader's ability to understand what is read. Readers should be better able to separate fact from opinion, substance from rhetoric, and become better consumers of information in our media-centered culture.

This volume of the Opposing Viewpoints Series does not advocate a particular point of view. Quite the contrary! The very nature of the book leaves it to the reader to formulate the opinions he or she finds most suitable. My purpose as publisher is to see that this is made possible by offering a wide range of viewpoints that are fairly presented.

David L. Bender
Publisher

Introduction

"A fetus is no more a human being than an acorn is an oak tree."

Caroline Lund and Cindy Jaquith,
Abortion: A Woman's Right, 1971.

"There is no abortion that is not the unjust taking of another's life."

James T. Burtchaell,
Rachel Weeping: The Case Against Abortion, 1982.

Few issues have fostered such contention and resulted in such polarization as has the topic of abortion. The participants in the abortion debate not only have firmly fixed beliefs, but each group has a self-designated appellation—pro-choice and pro-life—that clearly reflects what they believe to be the essential issues. On one side, supporters of abortion see individual choice as central to the debate: If a woman cannot choose to terminate an unwanted pregnancy, a condition which affects her own body and possibly her entire life, then she has lost one of her most basic human rights. These proponents of abortion believe that while the fetus is a potential life, its life cannot be placed on the same level with that of the woman. On the other side, opponents of abortion argue that the fetus is human and therefore endowed with the same human rights as the mother. Stated simply, they believe that when a society legalizes abortion, it is sanctioning murder.

Abortion is *not* just a contemporary issue. Historically, both tribal and urbanized societies have employed a variety of methods to end unwanted pregnancies. Germaine Greer in her book *Sex and Destiny* described some of the abortion methods used throughout the world. They include the application of pressure outside the womb—using logs and rocks and jumping on the woman's abdomen—as well as internal methods such as the ingestion of highly toxic chemicals and the use of various implements inside the uterus. In today's more industrialized societies, technology has simplified the abortion procedure to a few basic, safe methods. However, technology has also enhanced society's knowledge of the fetus. Ultrasound, fetal therapy, and amniocentesis graphically reveal that complex life exists before birth, and it is this potential—and many say actual—human life that is at the heart of the debate.

Anyone seeking material for a book on abortion can find literally thousands of articles, newsletters, and books on the topic. The issue is evident in radio, television, newspapers, magazines, nonfiction, and even fiction books. But the selection process is complicated by the overwhelming sensitivity the issue generates for people. Deep-seated views on both sides make the task of compiling an unbiased book on abortion a complicated and touchy one.

The editors of *Abortion: Opposing Viewpoints* have attempted to collect the most representative arguments on the abortion debate. They have endeavored to include prominent pro-life and pro-choice publications and authors who write from conviction, and, in many cases, from personal experience.

The issue of abortion, perhaps more so than most others today, finds few advocates taking the proverbial "middle ground." It is this polarity that makes abortion particularly suited to the opposing viewpoints approach. The five key topics debated are: When Does Life Begin? Should Abortion Remain a Personal Choice? Is Abortion Immoral? Can Abortion Be Justified? Should Abortion Remain Legal? As readers examine the highly charged viewpoints in this book, they will be faced with many thought-provoking and perhaps unsolvable questions about the nature of life. One matter seems certain: As long as contraceptives are not completely reliable and safe, or men and women neglect their use, abortion will remain an issue.

When Does Life Begin?

Abortion

Chapter Preface

Much of the controversy concerning abortion focuses on the question, when does human life begin? Some of the most common theories are that life begins at conception, at the first sign of brain activity, or at viability, when the fetus can survive on its own. Many Americans maintain that life begins at conception. According to abortion opponent John C. Willke, president of the National Right to Life Committee, "At the union of sperm and ovum there exists a living, single-celled, complete human being." Willke maintains that the laws of natural science prove that human life, complete and intact with forty-six chromosomes, begins at fertilization. Therefore, abortion at any stage of pregnancy is the immoral taking of human life and should be illegal.

In contrast, other Americans often assert that human life begins when a fetus reaches the age of viability, or is able to survive outside the womb. Celeste M. Condit, author of *Decoding Abortion Rhetoric*, for example, believes that prior to viability, the fetus is at an immature stage of physical and mental development and cannot be considered a human life. "The fetus before viability is not individually capable of life," Condit writes. "What the fetus requires is *the substance* of the mother's body." On this basis, Condit explains, abortion is moral prior to viability and should therefore be legal.

Many experts, including philosophers, scientists, theologians, and physicians, have pondered the question of when life begins. The authors of the following chapter present arguments in this continuing debate.

> *"I accept what is biologically manifest—that human life commences at the time of conception."*

Human Life Begins at Conception

Landrum B. Shettles and David Rorvik

Landrum B. Shettles holds Ph.D. and M.D. degrees from Johns Hopkins University in Baltimore, Maryland. For twenty-seven years he was the attending obstetrician-gynecologist at Columbia-Presbyterian Medical Center in New York City. He specialized in research in fertility, sterility, and diseases of newborn infants. He first discovered and distinguished between male- and female-producing sperm, and pioneered research in in-vitro fertilization. David Rorvik is a former science and medical reporter for *Time*, a weekly newsmagazine. He won a Pulitzer Traveling Fellowship. In the following viewpoint, the authors argue that there is one fact that no one can deny: The life of biological human beings begins at conception.

As you read, consider the following questions:

1. Why do the authors reject the idea that the fetus is only a potential life?
2. Why do Shettles and Rorvik believe that the unborn is "always a distinct human being"?
3. Why do the authors oppose abortion?

Most of the billions of cells that collectively make up a human being are "soma" (Greek for "body") cells. Unless manipulated in exotic ways, these body cells are and remain just what they appear to be: skin, hair, bone, muscle, and so on. Each has some worthy, special function in life, a function that it dutifully, if narrowly, performs until it dies. And the soma cells *do* die, ultimately leaving nothing of themselves behind.

There are some other, far rarer cells, however—known as "germ" cells or "sex" cells—that have the power not only to extravagantly transform themselves, giving rise to *every* other kind of human cell, but also to seize for themselves a bit of the "impossible": immortality. The sex cells are the sperm cells in the male and the egg cells in the female. It is only in combination, one with the other, that these cells can work their special magic, rise above the humdrum stasis of their somatic siblings, and confer something of their essences upon the future generations in which they will thus perpetuate themselves.

There is an "essence" in every cell, whether somatic or germinal, consisting of the nucleic acids, principally deoxyribonucleic acid—better known as "DNA," the basic stuff that forms the "building blocks" of life, the genes and chromosomes. Actually the genes are made up of much smaller units, so numerous that if you were by some miracle able to completely "unravel" the strands of DNA that exist in a single human being the "chain of life" would stretch across some millions of miles. There are many thousands of genes in the nucleus (central core) of each cell; these are arranged in larger chromosomal units, of which there are forty-six in each human body cell. The individual sex cells, sperm and egg, on the other hand, contain only half that number: twenty-three chromosomes each. It is only through combination, through merger, that the sex cells attain the full complement of hereditary units that defines a human being. . . .

The Merging of Egg and Sperm

The merger [of egg and sperm] is complete within twelve hours, at which time the egg—which may have "waited" as many as forty years for this moment—is fertilized and becomes known technically as the "zygote," containing the full set of forty-six chromosomes required to create new human life. Conception has occurred. The genotype—the inherited characteristics of a unique human being—is established in the conception process and will remain in force for the entire life of that individual. No other event in biological life is so decisive as this one; no other set of circumstances can even remotely rival genotype in "making you what you are."

Conception confers life and makes that life one of a kind. Unless you have an identical twin, there is virtually no chance, in the natural course of things, that there will ever be "another you"—not even if mankind were to persist for billions of years. Indeed, given the vast number of combinations possible among chromosomes, genes, and their smaller subparts, there is virtually no chance that even your own parents could ever come up with another "copy" of you, not even if by some magic they could produce millions of offspring. . . .

A Missouri Law's Definition of Life

1. The general assembly of this state finds that:

(1) The life of each human being begins at conception;

(2) Unborn children have protectable interests in life, health, and well-being;

(3) The natural parents of unborn children have protectable interests in the life, health, and well-being of their unborn child.

2. Effective January 1, 1988, the laws of this state shall be interpreted and construed to acknowledge on behalf of the unborn child at every stage of development, all the rights, privileges, and immunities available to other persons, citizens, and residents of this state.

Missouri House Bill Number 1596, passed in 1986.

Many who have studied the data regarding twins have declared themselves awed and astounded by the evident, sometimes overwhelming power of heredity. Even twins who have grown up in radically different home environments have exhibited, upon observation in later life, astonishing behavioral similarities. A significant number are found to have adopted remarkably similar lifestyles, often choosing the same occupations, marrying women who are alike in too many particulars to be accounted for by coincidence alone, and so on. The genotype that is conferred at conception does not merely start life, it *defines* life.

Conception sets in motion a series of events within the womb more complex and wondrous than anything that will ever happen to the body outside the womb. So astonishing are the happenings that transpire in the first moments, days, weeks, and months of life-before-birth that when we come to understand them fully we will very likely possess the answer to such puzzles as cancer and the aging process. By fully understanding life we will almost certainly be able to better understand death. . . .

Fascinating and purposeful though the sex cells are, ova and spermatozoa do *not* by themselves constitute human life. The sex cells are "half worlds" which only become whole in combi-

19

nation with each other—through the process I have described. This process helps to ensure, through its nearly infinite recombinant genetic possibilities, the continued variability, adaptability, and development of the species. It may seem that I am belaboring the obvious; but the question does have some bearing on the abortion debate.

Some pro-abortionists of the "life-is-a-continuum" school of thought have attempted to belittle the significance of the human zygote (fertilized egg), claiming it is no more worthy to be considered human life than is a single egg or sperm cell. Indeed, some go so far as to claim that if you can call the zygote human life, then you can call every other cell in the body human life as well. . . .

There may be some arguing in this fashion who earnestly believe that they have perceived a chink in the anti-abortion position, but most, I am convinced, are being disingenuous. . . .

There is another argument sometimes raised by the pro-abortionists that should be dealt with here. The fact that a significant number of zygotes fail to implant and therefore do not result in pregnancy is seized upon by a few as "evidence" that "even Mother Nature" does not consider the fertilized egg genuine human life, any more than "she" does the hundreds of thousands of eggs and millions of sperm that are "wasted." To this I can only answer that there are also a significant number of one-year-old infants who will never make it to old age, to puberty, or even to their second birthday. . . . Does the fact that life is interrupted at some point after it has begun mean that it never existed? . . .

A Distinct Entity

It should be understood that though I use different terms to describe the unborn—*zygote, embryo, fetus*—these labels do not reflect distinctly different phases of development; these terms are used as a matter of convenience to describe general changes. Some describe the "zygote" as becoming the "embryo" at the time of implantation; others say the "embryo stage" begins in the third week of pregnancy. Some say the "fetal stage" begins in the fifth week of development; others say the eighth week, and still others say the embryo does not become the fetus until the end of the first trimester. It is my view that once the major processes of differentiation are largely complete, the embryo becomes the fetus. That occurs by the end of the eighth week.

Whatever the terminology, the unborn is *always* a distinct entity, an individual human life in its own right and not simply some "disposable part of the mother's body," as some pro-abortionists argue. Fetologist Albert W. Liley has asserted: "It is the fetus who is in charge of the pregnancy." Even some who oppose restrictions on abortion would readily agree. For example,

Daniel Callahan, director of the Institute of Society, Ethics and the Life Sciences, has stated: "Genetically, hormonally and in all organic respects save for the source of its nourishment, a fetus and even an embryo is separate from the woman.". . .

The Time of Conception

I have learned from my earliest medical education that human life begins at the time of conception. . . . I submit that human life is present throughout this entire sequence from conception to adulthood and that any interruption at any point throughout this time constitutes a termination of human life.

Alfred M. Bongioanni, in *Abortion: Toward an Evangelical Consensus*, 1987.

I cringe whenever I hear someone utter the phrase, "It's just a blob," which the pro-abortionists frequently use to refer to the fetus in the first and even the second trimesters of development. Even some pro-abortion scientists refer to the fetus, at this and later stages, as "a mass of cells" or "mere tissue," in efforts to justify not only the abortion, but even also experimentation on the unborn. Some who employ this terminology are genuinely ignorant of the facts; some others, I suspect are willing to overlook the biological facts, convinced that abortion is an acceptable means to a desired end. . . .

My Position

I oppose abortion. I do so, first, because I accept what is biologically manifest—that human life commences at the time of conception—and, second, because I believe it is wrong to take innocent human life under any circumstances. My position is scientific, pragmatic, and humanitarian. My definition of man. . . is purely biological. Biological man is the product of the forty-six chromosomes that combine to confer a unique identity at the time an egg is fertilized by a sperm. I am not qualified to address issues of soul and spirit in any detail. It is my assumption, based entirely on faith, not science, that to the extent that biological man is imbued with a soul, he acquires that property at the moment of conception.

I reject all the arguments which seek to justify abortion on grounds that the unborn is not a living being or is somehow less than human, mere "potential life," or part of a "continuum of life that has neither beginning nor end." I resist and reject the new ethic which—even when it recognizes that the unborn child is not only human life, but meaningful human life—still considers that life expendable under many circumstances. The pragmatism that this ethic purports to embrace is, in my view, illusory; an ethic that makes any class of individuals expendable "in the interests of society" ultimately imperils that entire society.

I have always opposed abortion, except in those cases where the life of the woman is genuinely endangered by a continuation of the pregnancy. For some time, however, my position was one of "passive resistance." It was not until the 1973 Supreme Court decision that I made a public statement opposed to abortion. . . .

It comes as a surprise to some of my associates that I oppose abortion particularly since I pioneered some of the technology that made the so-called test-tube babies a reality. Because some of those who have opposed abortion have also opposed the creation of human life in the laboratory, the assumption has often been made that I would automatically be *pro-abortion*. Thus, I've learned a good deal about stereotyping. Now that I've made my anti-abortion views known, some seem to think that, "in order to be consistent," I will also become Catholic, vote for "hard-line conservatives," oppose civil rights, birth control, and education and adopt some anti-feminist views. At the very least some seem to expect me to account for my new outspokenness by declaring that I "saw the light" as a result of mystical religious experience. After all, I am told, "Everyone knows that abortion is a religious issue."

Being Anti-Abortion

In truth, there are some—a very few, in my experience—on the pro-abortion side who would like to see me embrace this stereotype. But I refuse to become wedded to either a conservative or a liberal political and ideological stereotype.

Far from being inconsistent with "liberal" or "humanist" principles, I believe that abhorrence for abortion squares precisely with those values. I believe that the clearest-headed pragmatists and "situational ethicists" *must* oppose abortion if they truly do prize the "greatest good for the greatest number." The Golden Rule is pragmatism of the highest order.

As for my position on abortion in my own medical practice, I try not to preach or proselytize. If a couple comes to me seeking an abortion or advice on abortion, I am pleased to be able to present my viewpoint. But for the most part, my approach is to show rather than to tell. I show the woman or the couple pictures of the unborn at various stages of development, explain what we know about the fetus at critical stages, and then let the parent or parents make up their own minds. If presenting the facts in an objective manner makes me guilty of attempting to "bias" the decision, then I stand guilty as charged.

We do well to remember that behind the barrage of words that make up the raging debate, there are real people, real feelings, real hopes, fears, triumphs, and tragedies.

22

"The possession of forty-six chromosomes does not make a cell a person."

Human Life Does Not Begin at Conception

Frank R. Zindler

Formerly a professor of biology and geology, Frank R. Zindler is now a science writer. A member of the American Association for the Advancement of Science, the American Chemical Society, and the American Schools of Oriental Research, he is also co-chairperson of the Committee of Correspondence on Evolution Education and Director of the Central Ohio Chapter of American Atheists. In the following viewpoint, Zindler argues that in order to be a human, a fetus must have a personality. Since it obviously lacks a personality, its rights should in no way supersede those of a pregnant woman.

As you read, consider the following questions:

1. What is the author's view of abortion as a contraceptive?
2. How many conceptions end in spontaneous abortion, according to the author? How does this support the author's argument that a fetus is not a human?
3. How would illegal abortion "subordinate the rights of actual persons to the imagined rights of eggs," according to Zindler?

Frank R. Zindler, "An Acorn Is Not an Oak Tree," *American Atheist*, August 1985. Reprinted with the author's permission.

When the Supreme Court of the United States of America decided on January 22, 1973, that women have a right to control their own reproductive destinies, it struck down the state laws which had made early abortions illegal. This allowed women to take a great step forward in their quest for social equality with men. Unfortunately, the Court was not as well-informed on the scientific and philosophical issues as it might have been, and although it came to what I consider to be the right conclusions, it did so partly for the wrong reasons.

While the Supreme Court did recognize the importance of the question "Is the fetus a person?" it was unable to break away from the irrelevant question "When does life begin?" Consequently, the Court's deliberations were hampered by an incorrect formulation of the central question at issue. Clearly, the question does not concern the beginning of "life." The unfertilized egg is alive, the sperm is alive, and no one has ever suggested that live babies result from dead sperm or eggs. Human life is part of a living continuum stretching back to the dawning days of the planet.

Despite the shaky scientific foundations of its decision, the Court made a statement of great practical utility. It declared, in effect, that during the first trimester of pregnancy, when abortion is far safer for a woman than is childbirth, essentially no restrictions can be placed upon a woman's right to privacy and upon her right to refuse to provide room and board for an uninvited guest. During the second trimester also, a woman's rights overshadow the "rights" of the fetus. During this period, the state may regulate abortion, but only to provide for the well-being of the woman—not because of fetal "rights."

Only during the third trimester, when the fetus becomes "viable"—capable of surviving on its own outside the mother's body—does the state begin to have a legitimate interest in the "rights" of the unborn. Even so, the mother's health is judged to be of greater importance than the life of the fetus.

Questions on Abortion

Since the legalization of abortion in America, a hurricane of opposition has developed. The most backward religious groups, Protestant as well as Catholic, have rallied to the appealing "Right-to-Life" slogan. No contrary slogan of equal appeal has yet been invented. "Freedom of Choice" just doesn't cut the mustard. "Life with Dignity" is so-so, and there don't appear to be any others. Thus, to oppose these fanatics is to appear to be anti-life and against rights. The "wrong" of right-to-life is not always easy to see.

Increasingly, ethically-concerned people have looked . . . for answers to the questions raised by believers in single-celled people. Although the questions are too numerous to deal with in a single viewpoint, I have, in the lines which follow, dealt with a representative sample of the questions which have been asked in the course of both formal and informal—informal sometimes to the verge of riot—discussions.

Isn't abortion more a social problem than a religious problem?

Of course, abortion—like all aspects of human reproductive behavior and personal freedom—is a "social" problem. If the Roman Catholic Church and several of the more strident fundamentalist Protestant churches were not, however, trying to force their religious dogmas on society by force of law and constitutional amendment, women would find less opposition to their

---

Human Awareness and Life

The assertion that life begins at conception can be made only on religious, not medical, grounds. No one can prove that the soul does not enter the egg with the DNA from the sperm. However, just as life ends with brain death, so a strong case can be made that human awareness and consciousness emerge only when the brain is well on the way to full deveopment.

Howard H. Hiatt and Cyrus Levinthal, *The New York Times*, February 18, 1989.

---

quest for self-determination in the area of reproductive rights. Opposing freedom of choice in the matter of abortion is tantamount to advocating compulsory pregnancy after rape, incest, or contraceptive failure. In the matter of abortion, as with all "pelvic issues," most of the shackles which restrain human freedom have been imposed by religious groups, directly or indirectly.

But doesn't freedom of religion allow the Roman Catholic Church to speak out on moral issues and make known its unchanging opposition to the killing of unborn babies?

The Roman Catholic Church has the right to speak out, but it does not have the moral right to force its unprovable theological opinions on non-Catholics. Moreover, the term "unborn baby" is a misuse of words. By definition, a baby is an individual who has already been born. Before birth, the organism is called an "embryo" or "fetus," depending on the degree of development.

As for the "unchanging opposition" of the Roman Catholic Church, its all-out opposition to abortion dates only from the microbiological discovery of human eggs and zygotes in the nineteenth century and the abandonment of the Aristotelian views held by the church for centuries. A distinction was made between the "formed" and the "unformed" fetus. An unformed fetus contained no "soul" and received its soul only later on—*40 days after conception in males and 80 days in females!* St. Augustine accepted this idea and taught that abortion of the *fetus informatus* warranted only a fine, but abortion of the *fetus formatus* was murder. The distinction was sanctified by Gratian in his codification of canon law in 1140. The modern idea that the zygote (fertilized egg) has a soul and that abortion at any stage of development is murder derives from a modern, unsuccessful attempt by religion to adapt itself to scientific knowledge.

But doesn't the Bible teach that abortion is a sin?

The King James version of the Bible does not even mention the word "abortion," let alone condemn it or say it is murder. In Exodus 21:22 (New English Bible, NEB), it says:

> When in the course of a brawl, a man knocks against a pregnant woman so that she has a miscarriage but suffers no further hurt, then the offender must pay whatever fine the woman's husband demands . . .

That this is roughly the biblical equivalent of a parking ticket is clear when one realizes that a son can be *stoned to death* simply for being a glutton, a drunkard, and rebelling against his parents (Deut. 21:20-21).

Not only does the Bible *not* condemn abortion, the jealousy ritual described in the fifth chapter of the book of Numbers (intelligible only in the NEB translation) would appear to make Jehovah himself an abortionist. According to the quaint and superstitious procedure prescribed for determining if a wife has been unfaithful to her husband, after a woman drinks the "water of contention" containing magic ink washed off from a scroll of curses, she will suffer a miscarriage (spontaneous abortion) if she is guilty of adultery.

How can you say the Bible doesn't have anything to say on abortion? Doesn't the first chapter of Luke tell about John the Baptist leaping in his mother's womb after recognizing Mary's voice?

First of all, we may note that this fable has nothing to say about *abortion*. Second of all, this fairy tale is an obvious attempt to show the *miraculous* origins of both John and Jesus. If only a miracle can make a six-month-old fetus understand speech and practice gymnastics, it follows that a normal fetus can't do such things. Thus, only a miracle can give a fetus the characteristics of a person. A normal fetus is not a person.

The Human Fetus

But doesn't the fetus move, show sensitivity to pain, and have a heartbeat and brain waves?

All this is true, but this does not make the fetus a person. To be a person, there must be evidence of a personality. Dogs, frogs, and earthworms have all the characteristics listed, but that is insufficient to make them persons.

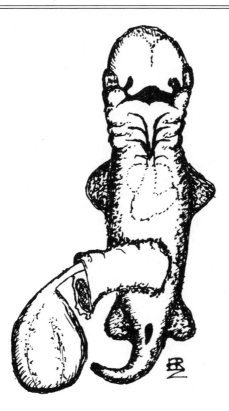

Figure 1. A five-week-old human embryo, drawn to eliminate the natural curvatures and to increase visibility of fish-like features. Easily seen are the gill-clefts, the two-chambered heart, the tail, the unpartitioned cloaca (anal opening), and the prominent yolk-sac (a reptilian feature).

Reprinted from *American Atheist,* with permission.

A brief review of human embryology is in order. It takes more than ten days after fertilization for the conceptus to become anything more than a hollow ball of cells at the stage of development of certain colonial algae. During the first week, it is free-floating and not even attached to the uterine wall. Not until the beginning of the fourth week does a heart begin to beat, and then it is two-chambered like that of a fish. Not until the end of the fifth week is there evidence of the beginning of formation of the cerebral hemispheres, and they are merely hollow bubbles of cells. Hemisphere development reaches reptile-grade during the fourth month, and primitive mammal-grade (opossum) during the sixth month.

Figure 1 shows the human fetus after five weeks of development. A prominent yolk-sac is visible, as if the embryo were that of a reptile developing within a yolk-containing egg. The heart is two-chambered like that of a fish, and in the neck region we see prominent gill-clefts. The arteries carrying blood from the heart to the gills recapitulate in minute detail the aortic-arch structures of fishes. Like the embryonic gills of fishes, the embryonic gills of humans lack the feathery respiratory tissues characteristic of mature gills.

This alleged person has two tiny, hollow bubbles of tissue for cerebral hemispheres, and it has mesonephric kidneys such as are found in fishes and amphibians. In fact, it still has traces of pronephric kidneys, the type found in the most primitive vertebrate known to science, the hermaphroditic hagfish!

Sexually, the embryo is indeterminate, still possessing an all-purpose anal opening, the cloaca. Although later in development this structure will become partitioned (into two separate openings in males, three in females), at this stage it is just like that of fishes. Just posterior to the cloaca is a tail which resembles the tail of a salamander.

Fetal Development

In the movie Silent Scream *a twelve-week-old fetus knows it's being killed. How can you deny the evidence of that film?*

As we have mentioned already, the brain of the three-month-old fetus is still at the reptile grade of development. It will be four weeks more before the cells in the cerebral cortex develop their characteristic six-layered structure, and only after that will the necessary nervous connections be made for processing of sensory inputs. At this stage, behavior is entirely reflexive, as in earthworms. Only long after birth will the nervous system be developed sufficiently for the perception of "the most mortal danger imaginable," to quote the narrator of the film.

On March 11, 1985, the *New York Times* printed an editorial critical of *Silent Scream*. Not only did the medical experts quoted by the *Times* confirm my opinion that the film showed nothing at all interpretable—that it was, in effect, a movie version of a Rorschach ink-blot test—the editorial revealed that a bit of fraud was involved too. According to Dr. Jennifer Niebyl of the Johns Hopkins School of Medicine, "right before [Dr. Nathanson] says the fetus is reacting and fighting aggressively, he has the film in very slow motion. Then, as the suction catheter is placed, he turns it on to regular speed. It's really very misleading."

Misleading indeed! The whole thing is just another religious hoax.

I agree that if the mother's life is endangered by pregnancy she should be allowed an abortion if it is needed to save her life. But I don't believe abortion should be a substitute for birth control.

We agree that abortion is a less desirable option as compared with contraception. But contraception often fails, and the same church which opposes abortion also opposes sterilization and contraception—thus creating a greater need for abortion than otherwise would exist. If one admits abortion to save a woman's life, one is admitting that the fetus is less important than the woman who incubates it. Once one has admitted this, one no longer has any grounds to accord full, legal personhood upon the fetus or—as extremists like Jesse Helms, Jerry Falwell, and Karol Wojtyla (alias Pope John Paul II) do—upon the fertilized egg itself.

Zygote and Soul

All right, I changed my mind. Abortion should not be allowed to save a woman's life. I think the soul does *enter the zygote at the moment of conception.*

If the single-celled zygote is *equal* to a full-grown woman, it follows that a full-grown woman can't be worth *more* than a single cell! Any one who values women so little is a menace to society and shouldn't be allowed to run loose without a leash.

With regard to "souls," there is no evidence that such things exist, let alone form a part of the fertilized egg. If a single soul inhabits a single fertilized egg, identical twins are in big trouble, since such twins result from the splitting apart of a single conceptus. Perhaps one twin has the soul of the zygote and the other twin is a soulless zombie! In some cases, one "twin" doesn't develop fully, and we have a two-headed or two-bodied monster.

Furthermore, modern biotechnological possibilities make the whole subject of "ensoulment" a laughable, medieval bit of theological befuddlement. It is possible to take two separate zygotes—each supposedly with its own "soul"—and *fuse them into a single conceptus.* Would the resultant single baby born after such fusion have *two souls?*

Potential Humans

But the zygote has forty-six human chromosomes and is a unique genetic being. It is at least a potential human being and should be protected as something very valuable.

The possession of forty-six chromosomes does not make a cell a person. Most of the cells of your body contain these forty-six chromosomes, but that does not make a white corpuscle a person! As for the significance of uniqueness, identical quintuplets are genetically identical, yet they have personal identities apart from their genetic endowment. The development of cloning will make the cellular offspring from a single zygote—all the cells being genetically identical—into a veritable army of genetically identical but different persons. Moreover, not every zygote contains forty-six chromosomes. Zygotes destined to develop into mentally retarded individuals with Down's Syndrome ("Mongolism") have forty-seven chromosomes, and a variety of other developmental defects are known which involve possession of fewer than forty-six chromosomes. Quite literally, such individuals are born without all their pieces! If possession of forty-six chromosomes makes something a person, then it would seem that possession of a different number would make something else.

As for potential human beings, an acorn is not an *oak tree!* With cloning, every nucleated cell in your body is a potential person. This being the case, brushing one's teeth should be a crime on a par with murder, since one destroys countless epithelial "potential people" with every scrape across the gums. *Fully one-third of all conceptions end in spontaneous abortion,* often at very early stages of development. Is god to blame for this? Should he/she/it be blamed for the destruction of so many "potential people"? And what of the case where the conceptus develops into a creature lacking a cerebral cortex?

Church Law

That not every conception leads to a "living soul" has been long recognized by the Roman Catholic Church. According to a 1954 edition of the *Codex Juris Canonici,* the Latin manual of church law, "Monsters and prodigies must always be baptized conditionally" (Canon 748, my translation). In other words, the church isn't sure if these things are persons—and in need of baptism—or not! The canon continues, "When in doubt as to whether one or more are persons, one is to be baptized absolutely, the others conditionally." At this point, the margin of my copy of the canon law has been annotated by some theology student of the past, "baptize each head absolutely."

So there you have it. Even the "modern" Roman Catholic Church admits that not every conception is a person. Not every abortion is "murder"!

As a clincher, we may mention the case where twins start to develop from the zygote, but one develops into a dermoid "nidus," a nest-like growth of hair, teeth, and mucous membranes. Not everything born of woman becomes a person. Potentiality is not actuality.

"The child in the womb . . . is an actual person, just like the rest of us."

The Fetus Is a Person

Stephen Schwarz

Many people, including Stephen Schwarz, the author of the following viewpoint, believe that the fetus is a person and should be treated with the same consideration as any child or adult. Schwarz maintains that personhood begins at fertilization and ends with death. The author, who opposes abortion, is a philosophy professor at the University of Rhode Island in Kingston.

As you read, consider the following questions:

1. How does Schwarz compare a person's physical growth with his or her identity?
2. In Schwarz's opinion, how is the unborn child both a potential person and an actual person?
3. According to the author, why do abortion rights advocates prefer to use the term "fetus" rather than "child"?

Excerpted from *The Moral Question of Abortion* by Stephen Schwarz. Used by permission of Loyola University Press, Chicago, Illinois.

The life of a human person is a single continuum, having different phases. Being a child in the womb is the first of these phases; further phases include being a newborn baby, a born baby in his fifth month, his second year, a child of eight, a young adult, a person in middle age, an older person. Life in the womb is part of life. Each of us can say, I was once a child of three; a newborn baby; a baby two months before birth; six months; and so on. Small children have a perfectly clear understanding of this, remarking, "When I was in Mommy's tummy . . ."

The core of the continuum argument is that the child in the womb is the same person as the born child he will become, as well as the youngster of six, the teenager, the adult, he will become later. I am now the same person I was ten years ago, even though I have changed. That "I have changed" means that I, the same person, have changed; these changes happened to me. I am now the same person who was once a newborn baby; and before that, a preborn baby in the womb. (*Person* means here simply "human being.")

I am now the same person as I was ten years ago. One way to understand this is through memory. I remember, not only events that occurred ten years ago, but myself experiencing these events. To remember an experience is to reach back, not only into the past, but into another phase of one's own life, the life of the same person.

The Meaning of Personal Identity

Memory of one's own past experiences presupposes oneself as experiencing them. I who now remember, and I who had those experiences, must be the same person. Memory can stretch no farther back than identity; I cannot remember an experience occurring before I came to be, for obviously such an experience was not my experience. But the converse is not true, for one's identity can, and does, stretch farther back than one's memory. That I cannot remember an experience does not mean it was not my experience. I cannot remember being born, nor any of the moments of my existence before birth. But each of these moments was a moment in my existence, a part of that continuum that is my life on earth.

The function of memory in the continuum argument is to provide a clear and vivid understanding of the meaning of personal identity. Suppose the being in the womb had mental capacities that were far more developed than they actually are. Then she could later say, I now remember experiencing such and such while in the womb. That is—and this is the crucial point—I now remember myself, *the same person*, having these experiences. That means of course that I was already present then. The ab-

32

sence of such developed mental capacities means the absence of such (actual) memory experiences; it does not mean the absence of the real identity that links the person as she exists now and as she existed then, and that is made intelligible by this (supposed) memory experience.

Already a Person

It is not so that there is something in the womb—"a blob of tissue" or a mere biological organism—that turns into a child. The child is already there, the same child, the same person all the way through. There are significant developmental changes, but these occur in the life of one and the same being who is present throughout; and who is the being to whom these changes occur. . . .

The person is already there in the womb: nothing needs to be added to make him a person. Indeed nothing can be added. For example, none of the suggested places to draw the line marks the addition of what is needed for becoming a person.

The Development of a Fetus

 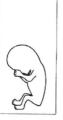   

4 WEEKS
The embryo is the size of a pinkie fingernail; the brain and the heart are beginning to differentiate. In the next two weeks, the digestive tract, sensory organs and arm and leg buds will begin to form.

8 WEEKS
Now measuring about 1 ⁄ inches, the embryo weighs about ⁄ ounce and its heart beats. Its ears and eyes are developing quickly; fingers and toes start to appear. The skeleton begins to harden.

12 WEEKS
The embryo has doubled in length to about 3 inches since the eighth week and weighs about ⁄ ounce. Reproductive organs start to form, and sex can be distinguished. After the third month, it is called a fetus.

16 WEEKS
The fetus undergoes a rapid growth spurt. It is 6 inches long and weighs almost 4 ounces. Fingerprints appear, and it may suck its thumb. Its lungs are formed but collapsed and functionless.

20 WEEKS
Now 8 inches long, the fetus begins to form eyelashes and brows; its eyelids separate. The woman may feel the fetus move. Its lungs, skin and digestive tract are not ready for life outside the womb.

Courtesy of Earthsurface Graphics.

Before concluding the continuum argument, two points of clarification are in order. First, the argument does not refer merely to the biological continuum of a single organism. Rather, it is the identity of a person through various phases of his existence. The biological continuity is certainly there, and it is an integral part of the continuum of the person. It is not the whole of it or its essence. The biological continuum is a dimension of the personal continuum, as the biological physical is in general a dimension of the human person.

Distinguishing Person From Nonperson

Second, the continuum argument is not the claim, often heard, that one cannot find a clear cutoff point in the life of a human being from conception to birth and beyond, a point marking the line between nonperson and person, or merely potential person and actual person. If there is a spectrum, say from A to Z, the fact that no clear, nonarbitrary cutoff point can be found along the way does not mean that A and Z cannot be radically different. Think of such examples as the color spectrum from black to white, or night to day. In each case A shades off into B, B into C, etc. There are no clear dividing lines; there is a continuity. But it is not the continuity of the continued existence of the same being; for example, a baby grows up to be a twenty-year-old, and always remains the same person.

If the continuum argument were merely that one can't find a clear cutoff point, it would indeed be invalid, and would not support the basic thesis, that the being in the womb is the same person who will later be born. Rejection of this argument does not touch the real continuum argument, the continuum of the same person. As already indicated, there is indeed no line to be drawn. The reason for this is the continuum of human life. Continuum implies no line; no line (by itself) does not imply continuum.

The child becomes an adult, and he is a child no longer. The fetus becomes the born child, and he is a fetus no longer. The stages—zygote, embryo, fetus, newborn baby, toddler, teenager—cease to be, but the person going through these stages continues to be, and continues as the same person. Being a fetus is merely one stage in the life of a person. . . .

An Actual Person

It is false that the being in the womb is merely a potential person. He is not a potential person, but an actual person, a fully real person, the same person he will later be. He is only smaller, less developed, in a different environment, and more dependent, in comparison to a born baby. Just as the small born baby is not a potential person but an actual person, so too is the preborn baby, who is simply a baby at an earlier phase of development. Both the postborn baby and the preborn baby are persons with potential, which is true of older children, and to a large extent, of all adults. We are actual beings with varying potentials for growth and development. In short, the child in the womb *has* potential, but he is an actual person, just like the rest of us.

Persons under anesthesia cannot feel pain, think, or communicate intentionally. That they cannot do these things means they cannot *function* as persons. But they have the *being* of a person. The child in the womb has a potential capacity to function fully as a person; in terms of being, the preborn is an actual person.

The greater the level of development, the greater the capacity to function as a person. Level of development is relevant only to functioning as a person not to being a person.

The Fetus Is Completely Human

In looking at abortion, the first question to ask is: What is this that grows within the woman? Is this human life? . . .

The answer lies in books on biology, embryology and fetology [the study of the fetus *in utero*]. In these sciences there is no disagreement on the facts of when human life begins. At the union of sperm and ovum there exists a living, single-celled, complete human organism.

John C. Willke, *Los Angeles Times*, March 3, 1990.

The term *fetus* is in itself a perfectly proper term, meaning "young one," and in recent times it has come to be understood in a very different, even an antithetical way, as something other than a person, a child. For some people it is a fetus instead of a child that a woman is carrying. It is psychologically easier to speak of the destruction of a fetus than of a child. Defenders of abortion object to the use of the term *child:* they generally do not want to appear as defending the killing of a child. So it is a fetus; destroying a fetus does not sound so bad. It is for this reason that it is imperative that we speak of the child and not the fetus. The reality of the child in the womb must be emphasized and conveyed to others.

Distinct Individuals

Suppose a woman suffers a miscarriage. A sympathetic doctor will not tell her, "You have lost your fetus"; he will say, "You have lost your child." If the child is marked for destruction he may well be referred to as a fetus, for this term has a cold scientific neutrality that effectively obscures the reality and preciousness of the small preborn child. . . .

A woman is walking down the street carrying a child in her arms. She is with child. Another woman is walking down that street. She is pregnant. She too is carrying a child, only in a different way. She too is with child, an expression often used, and most aptly, of a pregnant woman. The child carried in the arms is dependent, so is the child carried in the womb, only it is a different kind of dependence.

The woman and the child in her arms make two persons, two distinct individuals. The pregnant woman and her child also make two persons, two distinct individuals—one seen and one hidden from view, but each as real as the other.

"The fact that the fetus looks like a person does not make it a person."

The Fetus Is Not a Person

Michael Bettencourt

In the following viewpoint, Michael Bettencourt argues that the fetus is not a person because it lacks the ability to evaluate itself and to understand the physical setting of the womb. Bettencourt defines personhood as an awareness of both oneself and the world one lives in, a characteristic the author says is much too advanced for a fetus to have in its early stages of development. Bettencourt is a free-lance writer who lives in Manchester, New Hampshire.

As you read, consider the following questions:

1. How does Bettencourt define consciousness?
2. According to the author, why is the argument that the fetus is a person faulty?
3. What would be the outcome of declaring the fetus a person, in Bettencourt's opinion?

Michael Bettencourt, "Case for Fetal Personhood a Dubious Conception." Reprinted, with permission, from the September 20-26, 1989 issue of *In These Times,* a weekly newspaper published in Chicago.

The Missouri statute that the Supreme Court let stand in *Webster vs. Reproductive Health Services* declared in its preamble that life, and therefore personhood, began at "conception." While the statement appears to create a hard-and-fast medical benchmark, "conception" can mean several things.

Conception can mean fertilization, except fertilization can't be detected until the egg is implanted on the wall of the uterus. But while implantation can be detected hormonally, the egg can still "twin" in the early stages of implantation, so that if individuality is a key element of being a person, then one would have to wait about four weeks after the last menstrual period before saying that conception has occurred.

Some authorities believe conception has taken place when there is evidence of any of the following in the fetus: awareness of or responsiveness to outside stimuli, spontaneous muscular movement or a positive electroencephalogram (EEG)—all of which place "conception" still further along. So, if conception cannot be clearly defined, neither can the "personness" of the fetus—which hinges on conception—be indisputably demonstrated.

Like many arguments proposed by anti-abortionists, the "life begins at conception" argument does not draw a clear line. But anti-abortion proponents offer three others: appearance, ability to feel pain and potential.

Defining Consciousness

"Person" is often made synonymous with "human being," but a person is clearly more than simply a collection of cells created by 46 chromosomes (which is what a "human being" is). Often people on life-support systems are referred to as "vegetables." Clearly, while they *appear* to be human, having all the features and form of a human being, something is missing, something that might be called "consciousness."

While "consciousness" is difficult to define, its absence strikes us forcefully: the person has lost the ability to see the world and communicate about it and know what his or her place is in the scheme of things. Being a person involves having both consciousness (appraising the world in which one lives) and self-consciousness (appraising oneself.)

Awareness in this sense is not an automatic part of our genetic heritage. We have capabilities but are not finished products. Awareness must be earned in negotiation with the world, and this requires time for development, tension and thought. People are different persons throughout their lives, for each of our ages calls forth a different response. A person is a cumulative process, not something that is transmitted with the genes.

Anti-abortionists often avoid the topic of awareness, saying that the fetus is a person because it looks like a person (as a tactic, they will show pictures of aborted human fetuses that, not surprisingly, look human) and it can feel pain (and supposedly a number of other things as well). Mildred Faye Jefferson, an ardent pro-lifer, once said that "visuality equals truth."

Legal Dilemmas from Legal Protection

If fetuses are to be recognized as full-fledged persons, then justice requires that those who abort them for reasons less than self-defense must be recognized as full-fledged murderers and treated as such. Those who are rigorously opposed to retaining a policy of elective abortion on the ground that fetuses are persons must confront this implication sincerely and sensitively, and they must be explicit on what they are willing to accept as the practical implications of their position. If they are not willing to accept that those who abort should be subject to exactly the same treatments as others who murder innocent persons, then they do not *really* believe that the fetus has precisely the same moral status as you and I.

Joan C. Callahan, *The Ethics of Abortion,* 1989.

But the fact that the fetus looks like a person does not make it a person. Many animals with which humans are in contact have human-style responses and appearances, yet that does not make them persons and no one would argue that they were persons.

The appearance argument is not really an argument at all. Instead, it's a strong emotional identification with the fetus; the fetus can't reciprocate because it lacks the awareness to do so. Because the fetus looks like the people who are looking at the fetus, the fetus must therefore be like them. Add to this the strong affections attached to children and what emerges is, as one woman said at an anti-abortion lecture, the conviction that "in one's heart one knows the fetus is a person in the womb."

Pain and Sympathy

Thus the argument of the fetus as person, in this line of reasoning, comes down to an assertion that the "heart" (wherever that may be located and however it may work) knows what a person is and can determine personhood. The person who employs this argument is saying that the fetus is a person because he or she wants it to be a person but avoids the essential point of what makes that fetus a person. This is fine as a basis for private belief, but horrible as a basis for public policy, medical practice or law.

Many say that the root of the fetus' "personness" lies in its ability to feel pain, which was the basis for the highly erroneous video *The Silent Scream*. Many organisms feel pain, but feeling pain is not a way to determine what an organism "is." The fact the fetus can feel pain is not an argument for the fetus' personness because these incidents simply indicate that the fetus has a nervous system that feels pain. (In addition, the fetus' sensitivity to pain varies with its age; does that mean personness varies as well?)

We may, as many people do, sympathize with the pain we think the fetus feels, but we must be careful in saying that this sympathy establishes the personness of the fetus. It establishes nothing but our ability to sympathize.

The Potential-Person Argument

Others try to argue that because the fetus has 46 chromosomes it is a *potential* person and should be treated as such. Often this contention is stated in a highly dramatic way. This particular version comes from Garrett Hardin:

Two physicians are talking shop. "Doctor," says one, "I'd like your professional opinion. The question is, should the pregnancy have been terminated or not? The father was syphilitic. The mother was tuberculous. They had already had four children: the first was blind, the second died, the third was deaf and dumb and the fourth was tuberculous. The woman was pregnant for the fifth time. As the attending physician, what would you have done?"

"I would have terminated the pregnancy."

"Then you would have murdered Beethoven."

This story has two faults. First, it argues that blueprints are the same as the finished product. The expression of traits in a person is a very subtle balancing act between environment and genes; "who a person is," though dependent on genes, is in no way limited to them. Chromosomes are a necessary but not sufficient basis for personness. Beethoven, born in a different time and place (therefore having different blueprints), may not have become Beethoven. Second, the story could be twisted to say that we should encourage syphilitic and tuberculous couples to have as many children as they could in hopes of getting another Beethoven. This is absurd, but it brings out the emptiness of arguing about the potential person being lost. If Beethoven had been aborted, we would never know what we had lost, for we can't be aware of losing something we never had.

In fact, there are greater losses to mourn in this situation. Beethoven's mother, like most women, started life with about 30,000 immature eggs in her ovaries. She had only seven children. Therefore, 29,993 eggs never achieved personhood. Should we mourn that loss? And as for the father, the 100 million sperm he produced each day of his mature years—some 1 trillion in all—never connected with an egg. Does that constitute a loss in any meaningful sense?

In 1974 Garrett Hardin wrote a science fiction tale to illustrate why the fetus shouldn't be considered a person. He posed this situation: a 28th Amendment has been added to the Constitution, an amendment that gives the fetus all the rights to existence enjoyed by an adult. A lawyer is defending a client accused of murder under the 28th Amendment.

The lawyer is giving his final speech to the jury. After he has stated the reasons why his client did what he did, he has a demonstration to make to the court. As preparation, he gives background information on a new process of fertilizing eggs outside the womb so that they could be implanted in the wombs in infertile women. As he is speaking, he withdraws from a carton a flask of milky liquid containing, by his account, 20 trillion fertilized eggs. The flask was given to him by a doctor who specializes in the technique.

Fetal Rights Never Recognized

Despite its recognition of state interest in protecting potential life after viability, [*Roe v. Wade*] was explicit in denying constitutional status as a person to the fetus at any stage. The *Roe v. Wade* decision defended this position on the basis of both medical and legal history:

"In areas other than criminal abortion, the law has been reluctant to endorse any theory that life . . . begins before live birth" and has done so only "in narrowly defined situations and . . . when the rights are contingent upon live birth." The Court concluded this line of argument by saying: "In short, the unborn have never been recognized in the law as persons in the whole sense."

Catherine Gammon, *Present Tense*, September/October 1989.

The lawyer, to help the court grasp that number, compares it to the number of people who have ever lived on this Earth: 80 billion. The eggs he has in his flask represent 250 times the number of people who have ever inhabited the Earth. He goes on to say that by the 28th Amendment, each of these eggs is a full human being; therefore, he holds in his hand more people than have ever lived.

To make his point about the inadvisability of making the fetus a person, Hardin's lawyer places the flask on the judge's bench and says that he now turns them over to the court. It is the judge's responsibility to see that their lives are maintained. To willfully kill them would be murder; to allow them to die would be manslaughter.

The lawyer goes on to point out that each egg, if placed in a womb, will develop. How many of them could be developed that way? If, as the lawyer calculates, there are 1 billion women of childbearing age who might donate their wombs, would that be enough? No, because only one out of every 20,000 eggs would have a womb (assuming that the women would be willing to carry the eggs to term). For every egg saved, 19,999 would have to die.

Is there a resolution to this question of the personness of the fetus? No. At least, not if it's stated in the form of "Is the fetus a person or non-person?" A better way to think of the problem is: What are the social, legal, moral and economic consequences of believing one way or another? Looked at this way, considering the fetus a person can only lead to a situation in which the state forces compulsory motherhood on women, citizens become polarized, legal tangles beget legal tangles and the gap between rich and poor becomes wider than it already is. Ironically, declaring the fetus a person would destroy morality and cheapen the already precarious quality of life of many people, precisely the opposite situation envisioned by anti-abortion proponents.

Considering the fetus a person is a dead-end path and is in fact a distraction from the real issue at the heart of the abortion crisis: should women be forced by the state to be mothers, or should they be free to choose motherhood for themselves? Women, not fetuses, are the people we need to pay attention to.

"A conclusive answer to the question whether a fetus is a person is unattainable."

It Is Impossible to Know Whether the Fetus Is a Person

Jane English

The factors to determine what constitutes a person can be de-fined in many ways. In the following viewpoint, Jane English ar-gues that it is impossible to determine when the fetus becomes a person since there is no one definite set of such factors. En-glish also maintains that the gradual development of the fetus prevents pinpointing a time at which the fetus becomes a per-son. English (1947-1978) was a philosophy professor at the Uni-versity of North Carolina in Chapel Hill.

As you read, consider the following questions:
1. What factors make up our concept of what a person is, according to English?
2. Why can the author find no answer to the question of whether the fetus is a person?
3. According to English, how is the fetus both similar and dissimilar to a born person?

From *Canadian Journal of Philosophy*, vol. 5, no. 2 (October 1975): pp. 233-243. Reprinted by permission of the publisher and the author's estate.

The abortion debate rages on. Yet the two most popular positions seem to be clearly mistaken. Conservatives maintain that a human life begins at conception and that therefore abortion must be wrong because it is murder. But not all killings of humans are murders. Most notably, self-defense may justify even the killing of an innocent person.

Liberals, on the other hand, are just as mistaken in their argument that since a fetus does not become a person until birth, a woman may do whatever she pleases in and to her own body. First, you cannot do as you please with your own body if it affects other people adversely. Second, if a fetus is not a person, that does not imply that you can do to it anything you wish. Animals, for example, are not persons, yet to kill or torture them for no reason at all is wrong.

At the center of the storm has been the issue of just when it is between ovulation and adulthood that a person appears on the scene. Conservatives draw the line at conception, liberals at birth. In this [viewpoint] I examine our concept of a person and conclude that no single criterion can capture the concept of a person and no sharp line can be drawn. . . .

Criteria from Both Sides

The several factions in the abortion argument have drawn battle lines around various proposed criteria for determining what is and what is not a person. For example, Mary Anne Warren lists five features (capacities for reasoning, self-awareness, complex communications, etc.) as her criteria for personhood and argues for the permissibility of abortion because a fetus falls outside this concept. Baruch Brody uses brain waves. Michael Tooley picks having-a-concept-of-self as his criterion and concludes that infanticide and abortion are justifiable, while the killing of adult animals is not. On the other side, Paul Ramsey claims a certain gene structure is the defining characteristic. John Noonan prefers conceived-of-humans and presents counterexamples to various other candidate criteria. For instance, he argues against viability as the criterion because the newborn and infirm would then be non-persons, since they cannot live without the aid of others. He rejects any criterion that calls upon the sorts of sentiments a being can evoke in adults on the grounds that this would allow us to exclude other races as non-persons if we could just view them sufficiently unsentimentally.

These approaches are typical: foes of abortion propose sufficient conditions for personhood which fetuses satisfy, while friends of abortion counter with necessary conditions for personhood which fetuses lack. But these both presuppose that the concept of a person can be captured in a straightjacket of necessary and/or sufficient conditions. Rather, "person" is a cluster of features, of which rationality, having a self-concept and being conceived of humans are only part.

Absurd Question

The ancient Greek biology from which the original question of life arose is no longer scientifically credible. Today, for the most sophisticated scientists, the question "When does life *begin?*" is inadequate, meaningless, absurd, unanswerable.

Patricia Spallone, *Beyond Conception,* 1989.

What is typical of persons? Within our concept of a person we include, first, certain biological factors: descended from humans, having a certain genetic make-up, having a head, hands, arms, eyes, capable of locomotion, breathing, eating, sleeping. There are psychological factors: sentience, perception, having a concept of self and of one's own interests and desires, the ability to use tools, the ability to use language or symbol systems, the ability to joke, to be angry, to doubt. There are rationality factors: the ability to reason and draw conclusions, the ability to generalize and to learn from past experience, the ability to sacrifice present interests for greater gains in the future. There are social factors: the ability to work in groups and respond to peer pressures, the ability to recognize and consider as valuable the interests of others, seeing oneself as one among "other minds," the ability to sympathize, encourage, love, the ability to evoke from others the responses of sympathy, encouragement, love, the ability to work with others for mutual advantage. Then there are legal factors: being subject to the law and protected by it, having the ability to sue and enter contracts, being counted in the census, having a name and citizenship, the ability to own property, inherit, and so forth.

Now the point is not that this list is incomplete, or that you can find counterinstances to each of its points. People typically exhibit rationality, for instance, but someone who was irrational would not thereby fail to qualify as a person. On the other hand, something could exhibit the majority of these features and still fail to be a person, as an advanced robot might. There is no single core of necessary and sufficient features which we can draw upon with the assurance that they constitute what really makes a person; there are only features that are more or less typical.

This is not to say that no necessary or sufficient conditions can be given. Being alive is a necessary condition for being a person, and being a U.S. Senator is sufficient. But rather than

45

falling inside a sufficient condition or outside a necessary one, a fetus lies in the penumbra region where our concept of a person is not so simple. For this reason I think a conclusive answer to the question whether a fetus is a person is unattainable.

Here we might note a family of simple fallacies that proceed by stating a necessary condition for personhood and showing that a fetus has that characteristic. This is a form of the fallacy of affirming the consequent. For example, some have mistakenly reasoned from the premise that a fetus is human (after all, it is a human fetus rather than, say, a canine fetus), to the conclusion that it is a human. Adding an equivocation on 'being', we get the fallacious argument that since a fetus is something both living and human, it is a human being.

Historical Views of Personhood

Nonetheless, it does seem clear that a fetus has very few of the above family of characteristics, whereas a newborn baby exhibits a much larger proportion of them—and a two-year-old has even more. Note that one traditional anti-abortion argument has centered on pointing out the many ways in which a fetus resembles a baby. They emphasize its development ("It already has ten fingers . . .") without mentioning its dissimilarities to adults (it still has gills and a tail). They also try to evoke the sort of sympathy on our part that we only feel toward other persons ("Never to laugh . . . or feel the sunshine?"). This all seems to be a relevant way to argue, since its purpose is to persuade us that a fetus satisfies so many of the important features on the list that it ought to be treated as a person. Also note that a fetus near the time of birth satisfies many more of these factors than a fetus in the early months of development. This could provide reason for making distinctions among the different stages of pregnancy, as the U.S. Supreme Court has done.

Historically, the time at which a person had been said to come into existence has varied widely. Muslims date personhood from fourteen days after conception. Some medievals followed Aristotle in placing ensoulment at forty days after conception for a male fetus and eighty days for a female fetus. In European common law since the seventeenth century, abortion was considered the killing of a person only after quickening, the time when a pregnant woman first feels the fetus move on its own. Nor is this variety of opinions surprising. Biologically, a human being develops gradually. We shouldn't expect there to be any specific time or sharp dividing point when a person appears on the scene.

For these reasons I believe our concept of a person is not sharp or decisive enough to bear the weight of a solution to the abortion controversy.

a critical thinking activity

Understanding Words in Context

Readers occasionally come across words they do not recognize. And frequently, because they do not know a word or words, they will not fully understand the passage being read. Obviously, the reader can look up an unfamiliar word in a dictionary. By carefully examining the word in the context in which it is used, however, the word's meaning can often be determined. A careful reader may find clues to the meaning of the word in surrounding words, ideas, and attitudes.

Below are excerpts from the viewpoints in this chapter. In each excerpt, one of the words is printed in italics. Try to determine the meaning of each word by reading the excerpt. Under each excerpt you will find four definitions for the italicized word. Choose the one that is closest to your understanding of the word.

Finally, use a dictionary to see how well you have understood the words in context. It will be helpful to discuss with others the clues that helped you decide on each word's meaning.

1. Conception *CONFERS* human life, begins the growing process, and makes that life one of a kind.

   CONFERS means:

   a) prevents   c) increases
   b) gives   d) chooses

2. Some abortion rights advocates *BELITTLE* the significance of the fertilized human egg, claiming it is no more a human life than a single egg or sperm cell.

   BELITTLE means:

   a) praise   c) substitute
   b) appreciate   d) downplay

3. All overpopulated nations should promote contraception; it is one *PRAGMATIC* way to reduce the birth rate.

   PRAGMATIC means:

   a) practical   c) criticized
   b) foolish   d) complex

4. When a sperm cell fertilizes a human egg, they jointly *COMPRISE* the full genetic material necessary for a human being.

COMPRISE means:

a) contain
b) destroy
c) stimulate
d) separate

5. As a pregnancy progresses and the embryo grows, physical features once difficult to distinguish become increasingly *CONSPICUOUS.*

CONSPICUOUS means:

a) shaded
b) ugly
c) noticeable
d) hidden

6. In a mother's womb, the developing fetus will often move its own limbs. The fetus is acting of its own *VOLITION.*

VOLITION means:

a) speed
b) will
c) virtue
d) hunger

7. Abortion opponents believe abortion is the killing of human life. They say it is *IMPERATIVE* that people understand that the unborn child is alive.

IMPERATIVE means:

a) likely
b) mistaken
c) forgotten
d) necessary

8. Abortion rights advocates contend that laws banning abortion will deny women freedom of choice and cause *COMPULSORY* motherhood for some women.

COMPULSORY means:

a) complete
b) tedious
c) forced
d) legal

9. Not only does abortion harm women, it also *ADVERSELY* affects their families.

ADVERSELY means:

a) positively
b) unfavorably
c) aimlessly
d) smoothly

Periodical Bibliography

The following articles have been selected to supplement the diverse views presented in this chapter.

Joseph L. Bernardin — "The Consistent Ethic After 'Webster,'" *Commonweal*, April 23, 1990.

Daniel Callahan — "An Ethical Challenge to Prochoice Advocates," *Commonweal*, November 23, 1990.

Helen Cordes — "Re-examining Abortion," *Utne Reader*, March/April 1991.

Charles A. Gardner — "'Biological Destiny' Line Subverts Pro-Life Claims of Fetal Holocaust," *In These Times*, May 23-June 5, 1990.

Charles A. Gardner — "Is an Embryo a Person?" *The Nation*, November 13, 1989.

Christine Gorman — "A Balancing Act of Life and Death," *Time*, February 1, 1988.

Elizabeth Hall — "When Does Life Begin?" *Psychology Today*, September 1989.

Julia Kagan — "Prenatal Development and the Law," *Psychology Today*, September 1989.

Demetria Martinez — "Ethicist Says Brain Life Should Be Abortion Criterion," *National Catholic Reporter*, December 14, 1990. Available from PO Box 419281, Kansas City, MO 64141.

Margie Patlak — "Starting Point," *Los Angeles Times*, March 19, 1990.

St. Anthony Messenger — "Abortion's Evil Doesn't Depend on the Moment of Ensoulment," April 1991. Available from Franciscan Friars of St. John the Baptist Province, 1615 Republic St., Cincinnati, OH 45210.

William Saletan — "If Fetuses Are People. . . ," *The New Republic*, September 18-25, 1989.

Eloise Salholz — "Abortion's Dividing Line," *Newsweek*, October 23, 1989.

Joanne Silberner — "When the Law and Medicine Collide," *U.S. News & World Report*, July 17, 1989.

Peter Steinfels — "Catholic Scholars Widen Debate on When Life Begins," *The New York Times*, January 13, 1991.

2 CHAPTER

Should Abortion Remain a Personal Choice?

Abortion

Chapter Preface

When Becky Bell became pregnant in 1988, the 17-year-old Indianapolis student went to Planned Parenthood only to discover that she needed to obtain her parents' permission for an abortion. Bell feared notifying her parents and resorted to an illegal abortion. How she actually attempted her abortion remains unknown. What is known is that she developed pneumonia from the possibly self-induced abortion and died several days later.

Concerned parents and abortion rights advocates, such as the National Organization for Women and the American Civil Liberties Union (ACLU), argue that the fear of notifying parents can cause some minors to seek dangerous illegal abortions. According to the ACLU, "Becky Bell did what hundreds of thousands of women did before legalized abortion—she bought 'medical care' in the back alley." Adds Bill Bell, Becky's father, "The laws, the way they are now, prevented her from getting safe medical care. They are punishing these young women."

Abortion opponents argue that a minor's health is exactly why parental consent laws are justified. When 13-year-old Dawn Ravenell went to a Manhattan health center in 1985 for an abortion, she too had not told her parents of her pregnancy. But under New York law Ravenell was not required to have parental consent. Ravenell's abortion also ended in tragedy. After receiving an insufficient dose of anesthesia, Ravenell awoke from the procedure prematurely and began to vomit. A doctor gave her more anesthesia and inserted a plastic airway into her throat to ease her breathing. Alone in a recovery room, Ravenell awoke, vomited once again, choked on the airway, and had a massive heart attack. She died three weeks later.

Incidents such as these lead supporters of parental consent laws to argue that parents must be made aware of their daughter's planned abortion and its health risks, just as they are notified of other surgical procedures their child may undergo. "If a teenage girl must get her parents' permission to have her ears pierced," writes John Paul Wauck, "shouldn't parents have a say in a serious, occasionally life-threatening operation like abortion?"

While many Americans believe the abortion decision belongs to the affected woman alone, others believe that women should consult parents or partners. The authors in this chapter debate the issue of who should have a say in the abortion decision.

"I believe a woman is the proper moral agent to determine the use of her body; she should have the choice of carrying to maturity her pregnancy."

Abortion Should Remain a Woman's Personal Choice

George F. Regas

Abortion rights advocates argue that since the fetus develops inside the woman's body, and since the outcome of the pregnancy will profoundly affect the woman's life, abortion must remain a woman's decision. In the following viewpoint, George F. Regas firmly supports this position. He expresses his concerns about the 1989 Supreme Court decision in *Webster vs. Reproductive Health Services*, which allowed states to further restrict abortions. Regas rejects the court's opinion and favors an unrestricted right to choose abortion. Regas is rector of All Saints Episcopal Church in Pasadena, California. This viewpoint is adapted from a sermon given by Regas in July 1989.

As you read, consider the following questions:

1. How have politicians been misled by anti-abortion activists, according to the author?
2. When does life begin, in Regas's opinion?
3. What measures does Regas suggest to reduce the need for abortion?

George F. Regas, "A Priest on Abortion: Woman as the Proper Moral Agent," *Los Angeles Times,* August 6, 1989. Reprinted with permission.

Few of us are neutral about abortion. Most Americans want abortion to be legal and safe. They respect the freedom of a woman to choose whether or not she is to bear a child. But most Americans are concerned that we not create an abortion culture, that abortion not become just another method of birth control.

With 1.5 million abortions each year—4,000 a day—the issue becomes a profoundly pastoral one for me. I know children who are now with us because in the honest and prayerful struggle with the question of abortion, their mothers—some married, some single—decided to carry a child to maturity and birth. They all have expressed profound gratitude that abortion was a legal and safe option.

I know women whose lives were literally saved from unraveling emotionally and who were given a chance for healthy, mature living because legal, safe abortion was an available choice which they accepted.

As the fierce debate on this unyielding dilemma breaks across the American landscape, I want to share some of my convictions and my doubts. We are bound together by a community of faith. There is space for struggle, for conflict, for exploration, for listening and for loving those who disagree with us.

The Legal Issue

First, the legal issue. The Supreme Court's landmark ruling on Roe vs. Wade in 1973 made abortion on demand legal in the early stages of pregnancy and gave states the right to protect the potential life of the fetus in later stages of pregnancy—or, as the court said, when the fetus is viable, capable of living outside the womb. The medical and scientific communities have consistently said a fetus is viable no earlier than 24 weeks.

Then on July 3, 1989, a divided Supreme Court opened the way for states to limit a woman's access to abortion—allowed states to place more and more limitations on abortion. This decision did, however, stop short of overturning the Roe vs. Wade ruling that made the practice of abortion legal in America.

Associate Justice Harry A. Blackmun, author of the 1973 ruling, called the July 3 decision ominous. He wrote, "I fear for the future. I fear for the liberty and equality of millions of women. . . ." He said a woman's fundamental right to choose abortion had survived but it wasn't secure.

The July 3 ruling is an attempt to force abortion policy out of the courts and into the political arena—into 50 state legislatures. Associate Justice Antonin Scalia wrote that abortion is "a political issue" more than a legal one. So from now on state legislators will grapple with ethical, medical and legal complexities that even the Supreme Court couldn't solve. Walter Dellinger, professor of law at Duke University, said, "Virtually all the power in legislatures is held by men who will never be affected by the restrictions they impose." Yet their conclusions will have a profound effect upon one of the most intimate decisions in a woman's life.

© Taylor/Rothco. Reprinted with permission.

There is a story of three professional people arguing about whose was the first profession on Earth. The argument involved a surgeon, an architect and a politician. The surgeon said, "I had to be first. The Bible says that out of the side of Adam, God took a rib and created Eve. That takes a competent surgeon." The architect said, "No, you are wrong. I had to be first because the Bible says that out of the chaos God created and fashioned this marvelous universe." The politician said, "Oh no. I was first. Who do you think created the chaos?"

The Politicians Are Wrong

Politicians in the Missouri legislature are saying, "The life of a human being begins at conception." They will require a test at 20 weeks to determine whether the fetus is viable, even with the medical community agreed that all evidence says a fetus isn't viable before 24 weeks.

This is playing to the anti-abortionist position that abortions are being done very late. Politicians have been convinced that late-term abortions are commonplace enough to warrant restrictive legislation. Some anti-abortion activists have cleverly created the myth that women have abortions right up to the time of delivery for frivolous reasons. The facts are clear and otherwise: 90% of all abortions are done before the 13th week of pregnancy; fewer than 1% of all abortions occur after the 20th week —and most of those are for urgent medical reasons.

Missouri is one of many states that restrict funding for most abortions—leaving poor women and many young teenagers to scrape together enough money to terminate unwanted pregnancies. Only New York, California and a few other states provide funds for abortion. Now Missouri says no public facilities can be used. It hits the poor the hardest; the rate of abortion among women whose family annual income is at or below the poverty line is more than double the rate for women of the middle class and above. Some states also seek to ban abortions from all clinics and require a hospital setting. Now, more than 80% of abortions are safely and inexpensively performed in clinics. This hospital requirement would quadruple the cost to about $800 —one more effort to make abortion less accessible, especially to the poor.

Women and the Constitution

The Constitution guarantees a woman the right to exercise some control over her unique ability to bear children. The high court has now removed portions of that control. On the steps of the Supreme Court, Faye Wattleton, president of Planned Parenthood, asked rhetorically about these constitutional guarantees: "When did it become a political question whether women had reproduction rights?" The answer was easy: July 3, 1989. And yet as the late Associate Justice Robert H. Jackson said at mid-century, "One's right to life, liberty and property . . . depends on the outcome of no election."

Whether pro-choice or anti-abortion, you do not have the right in this diverse, pluralistic society to force beliefs and opinions on others. There can never be a just law requiring uniformity of behavior on the abortion issue.

From my perspective that is what the Roman Catholic Church and the religious right attempt to do on abortion. The late Cardinal Cushing of Boston once said, referring to the birth-control controversy: "Catholics do not need the support of civil law to be faithful to their religious convictions, and they do not seek to impose by law their moral view on other members of society." May his spirit prevail.

Many of us have deep religious feelings about abortion, about the moral quality of the individual decision involved; but I believe it is critical to distinguish how I might judge the act of abortion morally and what I believe a societywide policy on abortion should be. Whatever my views, the woman must be the moral agent in that decision.

The moral issue is the sanctity of life. The reason debate is so acrimonious is that both sides share the ethical principle of respect for life. But the sanctity of life doesn't end debate for we must deal with two sanctities—fetus and mother.

Let me state two extremes of the debate. Anti-abortion forces are declaring more and more that human personhood begins at conception—then aborting a fetus is, to them, no more acceptable than any other form of murder. . . .

Extremes Fall Short

At the other extreme, some pro-choice forces feel a fetus is a mass of dependent protoplasm to be extracted without regret. Abortion is merely the flushing away of a mass of tissue.

Both extremes fall short.

When does human life begin? When is there a living human person? That is not a biological fact to be discerned; it is a theological perception. To say the fetus is not alive, not a living reality, is absurd. From the moment of conception it is a growing life. But to say at the moment of conception there is a human person is equally absurd.

I believe there is life at conception, life at a special time in its development—part of a continuum that begins in the uterus, emerges as a human being at birth, passes through childhood, adolescence and adulthood and ends in death. The fertilized egg is human in origin and destiny. It is growing and has the potential of human personhood—though it cannot be called a human person at that early moment.

Such a distinction is basic even to conservative theologians like Dr. John R.W. Stott, who comments that the decision to abort for reasons of a mother's health involves a choice "between an actual human being and a potential human being."

Anti-abortion people want to erase all distinction between potential life and actual life.

For many women, abortion is one of the most important decisions they ever make. Two ethical concerns about life are present: the sanctity of the potential human person and the sanctity of a mother's life—her moral decision over her own body. She struggles with the quality of life she could offer the baby at birth, the impact of that birth on the existing web of her other responsibilities—plus her own mental health and well-being.

I am not pro-abortion—but I am passionately pro-choice. I believe a woman is the proper moral agent to determine the use of her body; she should have the choice of carrying to maturity her pregnancy. As a theologian I see no way the moral status of a fetus can be of greater moral standing than a woman deciding her destiny.

It is a question of individual conscience. I refuse to give over the moral issue of abortion to a church or the religious right.

Before 1973, American women often chose to risk their own lives rather than have an extra child that could destroy the family's ability to cope or would cause an unmanageable crisis in family life. Some ghastly practices were used when surgical, safe abortions were not available.

The radical nature of methods once resorted to speaks of the desperation involved in unwanted pregnancy. There is something vicious and violent about coercing a woman to carry to term an unwanted child. To force the unwanted on the unwilling, to use a woman's body against her will and choice, is a kind of legalized rape that is morally repugnant.

Let Women Choose

Even if I believe the fetus is human—and I do—it exists inside a woman's body. . . . Here, one human being is wholly contained within another. Rights are in conflict: the right of the unborn child to life against the right of the woman to decide what to do with a part of her body.

If a woman aborts her unborn child, some may define the act as murder. But if a woman is prevented from having an abortion by allowing society to take control of her body, she may feel imprisoned and invaded. . . .

Pro-choice women have accepted the moral responsibility for what they do with their own bodies—and the creature inside. One may not like their choice, but they have claimed the moral responsibility for themselves and said they are comfortable with it. Let them have it.

It is not healthy to mind someone else's business.

Kenneth Guentert, *U.S. Catholic*, April 1991.

The growing restrictions that state after state will place on abortion, in many instances recriminalizing it, will not reduce the instances of abortion. Women will continue to put their lives at risk to terminate unwanted pregnancy. New restrictions will only put poor women in a more desperate place and leave all women who have taken this risk more mentally scarred for life. I cannot believe such action reflects a moral society.

Is there a way out? As a priest and as an ethicist, I want to be counted as pro-choice, keeping abortion legal, safe and available to all. But I seek a society in which abortion is less and less necessary, so count me among those who favor public policies that will reduce the number of abortions without coercing women. The only way that is possible is to create a different kind of nation.

A New Society

• The society we seek must have as its primary agenda the rights of the born, the improved quality of life for those who come into this marvelous world—adequate care and protection from the first stirrings to the final groans. My grievance is severe with so many anti-abortion advocates who demand justice for the unborn but who also advocate dismantling social programs that provide a decent life for children once they enter the world.

If we are to reduce abortions, we must reaffirm by work and action the rights of the born.

• The society we seek doesn't flaunt and exploit sex at every turn. Vast numbers of adults today participate in the devaluing of human sexuality by separating sex from love and commitment.

• The society we seek is one where greater scientific effort goes into developing safer and more reliable birth control, along with a commitment to have this contraceptive information and these contraceptives available to all people. Today 50% of all teen-agers are sexually active. Only 33% of teen-agers use any birth control method consistently; 25% of all abortions are among the teen-age population. Condoms prevent pregnancy and protect against the AIDS virus. It's immoral not to act with urgency in getting contraceptives to teen-agers who are sexually active.

• The society we seek says all life is sacred everywhere, for if it is cheap anywhere, it is cheap everywhere.

Only as we see every human being across this planet as a sacred person to be cherished—only then will we see a society emerge in which abortion is less and less a necessary option.

So with hearts that feel and brains that think, let us continue to walk as disciples of the Christ. And for me, at this moment in time, that means to join my life in solidarity with women who claim the moral responsibility over their own bodies. May God direct our efforts and illuminate our path.

Amen.

> *"The abortion culture devalues . . . unborn children by turning them into objects of choice."*

Abortion Should Not Remain a Woman's Personal Choice

Maggie Gallagher

Those who believe abortion should not be a woman's personal choice argue that the fetus's right to life must be protected. In their opinion, to abort the fetus is to kill another human being. In the following viewpoint, Maggie Gallagher takes this argument a step further. She contends that the ability to make certain choices, particularly the freedom to choose abortion, is a disaster for women and children. For example, Gallagher argues that the freedom to choose abortion deprives women of the experience of childbirth and mothering, and in the process snuffs out the lives of their innocent babies. Gallagher is a former editor of *National Review*, a conservative weekly newsmagazine.

As you read, consider the following questions:

1. How does the author describe the 1973 *Roe v. Wade* decision?
2. How did having a baby affect Gallagher's views on abortion?
3. What is the "myth of abortion," according to Gallagher?

Reprinted, with permission, from *Enemies of Eros* by Maggie Gallagher; copyright © 1989 Bonus Books, Inc., 160 E. Illinois St., Chicago, IL 60611.

When I was in high school and much of college, I believed in all the cliches of my generation. I believed in reproductive freedom. I believed that abortion "cured" the problem of unwanted children, and that every child has a right to be loved and wanted. I believed that no one had a right to tell me what to do with my body. . . . I believed that abortion was a positive good: in time it would make all children one of the Chosen People. Over time, as I began looking at the choices open to me, I learned that for adults, choice is an overrated virtue; applied to children, it is a disaster. . . .

Children of choice are a new phenomenon, but not, as many people say, because of recent advances in contraceptive technology. Long before the Pill, married couples had exercised control over their fertility. Urban middle-class families in America have been limiting births for more than a hundred years. But only in this generation have we created the dangerous fantasy that planned parents are better parents and that "accidental" children are less valuable, less happy, less *wanted* than children who have been made to order.

Choice is the opiate of the liberal. . . . Where choice is, the sexual liberal believes, justice flourishes and happiness will reign. Children of choice will of course be the happiest children of all. You can see the beginning of this hallucination in adoption literature of the fifties which downgrades mere "biological" ties in order to reassure adoptive parents. It picks up steam in the political controversies over contraceptives in the sixties. But it did not become the ruling ideology until 1973, when the Supreme Court of the United States made abortion on demand the law of the land.

Roe v. Wade did the unthinkable. It re-established as a Constitutional principle an idea we thought died on the blood-drenched battlefields of the Civil War: that there can be human beings who are not persons.

The humanity of the unborn is not and cannot be an issue. Peering into the womb, scientific technology has settled a question our ancestors could only ponder: human life begins at the moment of conception. The fetus is alive and (being a human fetus) is human; it is a human being.

But what we have come to believe in the long years since seven Supreme Court justices took it upon themselves to inflict an abortion crisis on this country, is something else; something dark, dangerous, arrogant, and ominous: we have come to doubt that being a human being is enough.

Fetal Personhood

The debate over abortion has come to turn over the *personhood* of the fetus, just as feminism, as Betty Friedan wrote in 1981, is about "the personhood of women." A person is someone who cannot be sold into slavery. To kill a person is murder. What *Roe v. Wade* did is destroy the idea that all human beings are people. Since *Roe*, being a human being no longer gives you any human rights. Since *Roe*, you must meet some other vague and undefined criteria—the ability to reason, the ability to make choices, the ability to live on your own, the ability to make adults go oooooh and aaaah while they tickle their toes. Some ability, it's not clear what, earns for you the right to life.

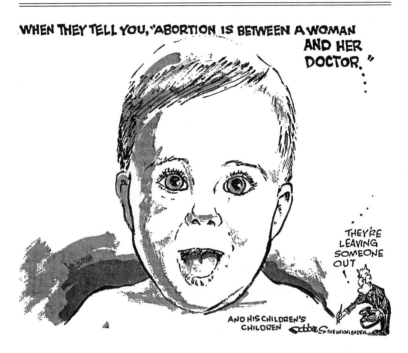

Dobbins/*Union Leader*. Reprinted with permission.

There is no rational distinction between a fetus and a baby. At some barely-suppressed level of consciousness many women know this. "Most women when they have an abortion don't really know what they are doing—they're either so young, so ignorant, or so frightened," one social worker at Abortion Hotline, a crisis counseling and referral center in Portland, Oregon, told me. "Down the line, five, six, or seven years when they have children, some kind of trauma almost always comes up . . . and down the line, most women do think of the aborted fetus as a living being, as a baby.". . .

On July 3, 1989, the Supreme Court took the first step in the long process of overturning *Roe v. Wade*. The debate unleashed by *Missouri v. Webster* already has engulfed the country. As the battle shifts to state legislatures, the debate over abortion threatens to preoccupy and divide the country like no other issue since the great civil rights struggles of the 1950s and 1960s. It is a debate over what it means to be a person.

Abortion devalues some human beings in defense of a frail and limited concept of personhood: the right to choose, and right to be one of the Chosen People. Abortion is both the necessary tool and the cultural embodiment of those who believe that families are formed by choice, that choice nurtures and sustains them.

Academics and activists who make choice the source of family obligation are struggling with the problem: how can woman be morally and legally held responsible for the great burden of caring for a child? This is the current answer: because she *chose* to have children.

A woman sufficiently alienated from her body might be made to believe it. As her belly swells with life and her breasts swell with milk, she might just be deluded into believing that it is her disembodied mind which connects her to her child. Then, like me, she will be in for a surprise. I was twenty-two and unmarried when my son was born, just a few months after I had graduated from Yale University. I remember sitting in the hospital bed, holding my tiny naked son. It came as such a shock to me, more powerful and yet akin to the shock of falling in love, this sense of absolute and unbreakable connection. At that moment, he was the most important thing in my life, and though I have endured, as other mothers do, the usual quota of baby messes, emotional aggravation, missed deadlines, and deferred gratifications, I have never doubted it since.

The Shock of Motherhood

Why hadn't anyone told me it was like this? They were too busy telling me (and I believed them) about my right to self-determination, bodily and otherwise. I have always been intensely ambitious. Before Patrick was born, I believed I did not want to have children. Once he came into my life, I found to my profound surprise that I wasn't going to let any ambitions of mine get in the way of caring for his needs.

I have since talked to many women of my generation to whom motherhood came in the same way: as an intense gratification, and an unutterable shock. I made the choice, as every woman must today in a society in which abortion is easily available and widely promoted, to give birth. But I never succumbed to the delusion that my measly little act of choice had anything at all to do with what I felt for my son.

The horror of abortion is not just that a woman destroys a child, but that a woman destroys *her* own child. We have a duty not to kill any human being, but we owe our children much more: care, protection, the effort of daily love. Abortion is the refusal to acknowledge the unconditional claim children have on our lives. In an aborted society, parental love is hedged in with conditions. I will care for you only if: it seems like it would be gratifying; if it doesn't interrupt my education; if it doesn't interrupt my marriage; if I have the time, and it doesn't interfere with my career; if you love me enough to make it worth my while.

We Must Choose Life

It is possible to get so caught up trying to be sensitive to the woman and her suffering that we forget the baby altogether. But weighing a woman's situation, no matter how tragic, against a baby's right to life only makes sense if we believe the baby is indeed a baby.

I *do* believe it is a baby, and this belief becomes more burdensome everyday. It is no longer acceptable to me to take a clever line about laws being ineffective and needing to change the world so that no woman ever feels an abortion is her only answer.

I can no longer say blithely that no one "likes" abortion and that the real solution is birth control. The situation is far too serious for such waffling nonstatements. Indeed, if I have learned anything from the pro-choicers, it is this: we have to choose between life and death.

Jo McGowan, *U.S. Catholic*, April 1991.

Every woman who has a child she loves knows the lie of abortion. Through the long months of pregnancy, the being that grows in the womb is not a blob of cells. The grief a woman who miscarries feels is not for a potential human being, it is for her baby. The careful euphemisms used in abortion clinics are evidence of the bad faith of the abortion culture. Women are never told (and orthodox feminists fiercely oppose laws requiring doctors to inform us) that the blob of cells may have tiny fingers, toes, a beating heart, and brain waves. Clinic personnel do not even refer to this developing human being as a "fetus"; nor is the word "abortion" used. It might be too painful for women to face what we are doing. So we are reassured. The nurse tells us "the procedure" will eliminate "the blob of cells" from the uterus. Then the "product of conception" (my personal favorite euphemism) will be disposed of. A day off, a few aspirin, and, presto, good as new.

The abortion culture devalues born children as well as unborn children by turning them into objects of choice. But it is not just children that are affected. I was a teenager in the mid-seventies when I first heard the argument that abortion could lead to infanticide and the killing off of the elderly. I dismissed it as absurd. Daniel Callahan did the same at more scholarly length in his influential 1970 book, *Abortion: Law, Choice and Morality*. But we were both wrong. It took less than fifteen years, but now retarded babies with birth defects may be legally starved to death. Old people, if they are unconscious or have other cognitive defects, may already be ordered killed by their relatives with the approval of a judge. . . .

Freedom to Choose Is a Lie

The force which drives our bodies together in lust and the force which binds us to our children are one and the same. Maternal love is an intensely sexual experience, more sexually-satisfying than any feeling produced by the manipulation of body parts. Far from freeing women's sexuality, abortion is an antisexual act. "To say that in order to be equal with men it must be possible for a pregnant woman to become unpregnant at will is to say that being a woman precludes her from being a fully functioning person. . . . Of all the things which are done to women to fit them into a society dominated by men, abortion is the most violent invasion of their physical and psychic integrity," writes New Zealand feminist Daphne DeJong. "It is a deeper and more destructive assault than rape, the culminating act of womb-envy and woman-hatred. . . ."

Many women who have had abortions know this only too well. Sexual relationships almost never survive an abortion, and a woman in love with her child's father who receives any encouragement from him seldom has an abortion. In turn, many women who have abortions report suddenly feeling sexually cold. Their bodies are not sources of pleasure or abundance, but of sexual rejection. Their lovers reject the fruits of their bodies, or they themselves do. It makes little difference, the result is the same. The femaleness of their body, their sexuality, has proven a tremendous liability. In their womb is death and the vagina is a pathway to it. How much better to be a man and permanently barren and therefore impregnable.

The myth of abortion is that choice sets parents and children free. Today, women alone choose to have children and, increasingly, women alone bear the responsibility for raising them. Choice is an escape hatch for men and a lie for women: a lie because giving life is a leap into the future for which nothing in the past can prepare one; no one ever knows in advance what raising children will be like.

But the obsession with carefully planned parenthood does serve one important social function; it keeps us from noticing some perfectly obvious causes of the current epidemic of battered children and broken lives.

"Parental involvement [in minors' abortion decisions] alerts parents to potentially dangerous physical and emotional problems of which they otherwise would be unaware."

Parents Should Participate in Teenage Abortion Decisions

Anne Marie Morgan

In June 1990, the U.S. Supreme Court upheld two state parental consent abortion laws: a Minnesota law requiring a minor to inform both parents of her intended abortion and an Ohio law requiring notification of just one parent. Many other states have such laws. In the following viewpoint, Anne Marie Morgan argues that these parental consent requirements are necessary to protect minors' health. Morgan maintains that in the event of complications following abortion, such as infection or heavy bleeding, parents and doctors will have been notified and thus be prepared to treat such problems. Morgan is a free-lance writer and contributor to *Chronicles* magazine, a monthly publication of conservative political and social opinion.

As you read, consider the following questions:

1. In Morgan's opinion, why are most minors not given pre-abortion counseling with a doctor?
2. Why does the author believe that most minors are not mature enough to make the abortion decision?

Anne Marie Morgan, "Alone Among Strangers: Abortion and Parental Consent," *Chronicles,* October 1990. Reprinted with permission.

At the moment the U.S. Supreme Court upheld the right of states to enact parental consultation abortion statutes, the abortion-advocacy organizations went into high gear. The *Hodgson v. Minnesota* and *Ohio v. Akron Center for Reproductive Health* decisions "endangered teens," they claimed, and NOW [National Organization for Women] President Molly Yard charged that the Court had "thrown down the gauntlet before the young women and girls of America." However, a rational—rather than emotive—analysis of the relevant issues reveals that the Court's decisions were very sensible ones. Notwithstanding the pained protests, the rulings should have a critical impact on whether young, frightened, pregnant minors will be the recipients of their parents' counsel or the abortionist's zeal, and whether the lucrative abortion-on-demand industry will continue virtually unrestrained.

Of the 1.5 million abortions performed in the U.S. annually, nearly one-third are on minors, many without parental consent or even *knowledge*. While state laws require parental *permission* for other surgery on minors, abortion has been the sacrosanct exception. Yet there is broad-based public support for parental involvement laws; for example, a 1989 *USA Today* poll reported that 75 percent believe parents should be notified before a female under 18 has an abortion. A nationwide *Los Angeles Times* survey of *women who have themselves undergone abortions* indicated that fully two-thirds agreed that "Minors should have to get their parents' permission before they can get an abortion."

Nonetheless, this is not the practice in most states. While 37 states have passed parental involvement statutes, until this Supreme Court decision most were temporarily or permanently enjoined. Other legislatures seeking passage became battlegrounds for bitter debates.

Intense Opposition

Why is there such intense opposition to laws that the public views as simply common sense? Privately, abortion advocates desperately fear that parental consultation laws mark the proverbial foot-in-the-door to overturning abortion-on-demand. Publicly, they offer an array of unsubstantiated objections.

Opponents' arguments can be examined in light of three compelling state interests for requiring parental consultation, as delineated in the High Court's 1976 *Bellotti v. Baird* decision: "The peculiar vulnerability of children; their inability to make critical decisions in an informed, mature manner; and the importance of the parental role in child rearing." Substantial documentation has emerged to sustain the Court's position.

Critics contend that parents are extraneous, since minors will have abortions "in consultation with their doctors." This is an exaggeration. Many young girls never see a doctor until they undergo surgery. Most abortions are performed at free-standing abortion clinics, *not* in hospitals, and nearly all states have repealed clinic regulations or licensure. Pre- and post-abortion counseling and emergency equipment are not required, and any doctor (not solely obstetricians) may perform abortions. Justice John Paul Stevens' concurring statement in *Danforth* in 1976 is correct: "The majority of abortions now are performed by strangers in unfamiliar surroundings, where minors are alone, furtive and frightened visitors subjected to assembly line abortion techniques." Dr. Edward Allred, who owns an abortion clinic chain that performs 60,000 abortions annually, described clinic practices for the *San Diego Union* in an October 12, 1988, article:

> Very commonly we hear patients say they feel like they're on an assembly line. We tell them they're right. It is an assembly line. . . . We're trying to be as cost-effective as possible and speed is important. . . . [W]e try to use the physician for his technical skill and reduce the one-on-one relationship with the patient. We usually see the patient for the first time on the operating table and then not again.

The absence of clinic regulations to protect women's health

Dana Summers. The Washington Post Writers Group. Reprinted with permission.

and safety encourages slipshod operations, including "abortions" on women who were not pregnant. The lack of emergency equipment has resulted in tragedy. While Debra L. was undergoing her abortion, she swallowed her tongue and attendants were unable to restore her breathing to normal. The clinic's director called Debra's mother to convey that her daughter had had "minor surgery" and was having "respiratory problems." Hospitalized, Debra lay in a coma for two and a half months, then died. Her mother, an amicus [friend of the court] in *Hodgson*, grieves that her daughter could have had an abortion without her knowledge.

Abortion-related Consequences

Opponents of parental notification say abortions are so problem-free that parents are not necessary, but evidence suggests otherwise. Scores of medical journals report that women under 18 who obtain abortions are more susceptible to physical injury, and have some of the most catastrophic complications.

The *Southern Medical Journal* cited adolescent case studies of abortion-related complications, including uterine rupture or perforation, cervical lacerations, hemorrhaging, pelvic pain, endometritis, incomplete operations, infertility, and repeated miscarriage. A typical pattern emerges with a minor's complications: she will delay health care out of fear of parental discovery of the abortion, and then go to a hospital emergency room. "The teenager, frightened and mentally and physically traumatized by her abortion, will often not seek help until she is almost moribund. Her parents may be the last to know." Ironically, she must have parental consent for treatment.

Dr. James Anderson, a Virginia emergency room physician, shocked even committed abortion advocates at the Virginia General Assembly when he testified of his hospital experiences. Dr. Anderson frequently treats minors who have had abortions (without parental knowledge) for severe post-abortion complications. He also observes the perilous adolescent pattern of delaying treatment. One patient died after becoming so infected after an incomplete abortion that antibiotics could not save her. Furthermore, a doctor faces a life-threatening dilemma in diagnosing a problem when a patient *denies* having an abortion due to fear of parental discovery—because proper treatment relies on accurate diagnoses. The physician must guess at the truth. Dr. Anderson testified he is often forced to break the news to parents.

Hodgson amicus Rachel E. manifested this "vulnerability." After undergoing a clinic abortion at 17 on the advice of her high-school counselor, she developed flu-like symptoms. Without post-abortion instructions, she assumed that these were unrelated. Although she finally went to her family doctor, she did not inform him of her abortion. Bacterial endocarditis, a result of a post-abortion infection, caused a blood clot, stroke, and coma. Rachel regained consciousness, but remains a permanently wheelchair-bound hemiplegic.

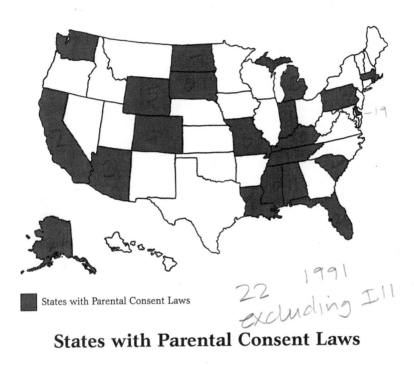

■ States with Parental Consent Laws

22 1991
excluding Ill

States with Parental Consent Laws

Source: Americans United for Life.

Clearly, parental involvement alerts parents to potentially dangerous physical and emotional problems of which they otherwise would be unaware. Emotional vulnerabilities can be equally critical. More minors than older women suffer severe anxiety, acute depression, long-term guilt, consternation, *and* attempted suicide following abortion. The latter is particularly compelling. In *Pediatrics* (1981), Dr. Carl Tishler alerts physicians to adolescent suicidal tendencies from "anniversary reactions"—on the perceived birth date had the baby come to term. One wonders how many adolescent suicides were young, grief-stricken girls whose parents were unaware that abortion triggered their despondency.

Demographic evidence refutes the charge that parental involvement will cause teens to postpone care and undergo more dangerous late-term abortions. Missouri, whose parental-judicial consent statute was upheld by the High Court, provides excellent data to evaluate the law's effect. For young women under the age of 18, the number of abortions done in 1984 (the last full year before the statute took effect) was 2,564, with 361 done after 13 weeks. In 1987, those numbers were 1,859 and 286 respectively. In other words, the number of second-trimester abortions among Missouri minors dropped by 20 percent after the statute's enactment. The number of Missouri's total minor abortions also declined—by 27 percent.

Reduction in Pregnancies

The claim that births to teens will increase with parental involvement is patently false. Minnesota's parental notice law was in effect for four years before being enjoined. Its data exhibit an unexpected benefit: a drastic reduction in minor pregnancies, abortions, and births. The 1986 Report of the U.S. House of Representatives Select Committee on Children, Youth, and Families entitled *Teen Pregnancy: What Is Being Done? A State By State Look* related that from 1980 to 1983, following enactment of a 1981 parental notification law, births declined 23.4 percent, abortions decreased 40 percent, and pregnancies fell 32 percent among fifteen- to seventeen-year-olds.

The *Minneapolis Star and Tribune* (April 20, 1984) reported:

> The surprise finding raises new questions about the effect of a parental notification law that went into effect between those two years. It also raises the possibility of some changes in adolescent sexual patterns. . . . "It would appear that women under age 18 are reducing their risk of pregnancy," [Paul] Gunderson [the Health Department's chief of statistics] said.

Danforth noted the historical and necessary legal limitations of minors:

> Because he may not foresee the consequence of his decisions, a minor may not make an enforceable bargain. He may not lawfully work or travel where he pleases. . . . Persons below a certain age may not marry without parental consent and they may not vote. . . . But even if it is the most important kind of decision a young person may ever make, that assumption merely enhances the quality of the State's interest in maximizing the probability that the decision be made correctly and with full understanding of the consequences of either alternative.

Opponents say the decision to abort should be left to minors.

70

But a 1989 *Los Angeles Times* poll of women who have undergone abortions indicates that one out of every four women (26 percent) "mostly regrets" her abortion. Such women subsequently experience profound grief.

Adolescents in particular manifest confusion about an abortion decision, changing their minds frequently. Abortion involves a severe double loss for some adolescents: fully 17 percent of minors who have abortions compensate for a first abortion by becoming pregnant again within one year.

Opponents of parental involvement laws wrongly argue that minors already notify parents. One study confirmed that 71 percent informed a best friend, while only 37 percent informed mothers and 26 percent informed fathers. In *Hodgson v. Minnesota* (1988), the Eighth Circuit noted the testimony of a clinic co-director: "Prior to the [parental notification] statute, approximately 25 percent of the pregnant women she counseled told one or both parents of their pregnancy and intended abortion."

In *Pierce v. Society of the Sisters*, the Court upheld the rights, authority, and responsibilities of parents over their minor children: "[T]he child is not the mere creature of the state; those who nurture him and direct his destiny have the right, coupled with the high duty, to recognize and prepare him for additional obligations." Other precedents concur, such as *Prince v. Massachusetts* in 1944: "[P]arents. . . who have the primary responsibility for children's well-being are entitled to the support of law designed to aid discharge of that responsibility."

Opponents of parental consultation dismiss the significant issue of family integrity. Yet the parent-child relationship is a *permanent bond*, unlike that between an abortionist and his client, or between two teenage best friends. Research by Dr. Everett Worthington of Virginia Commonwealth University reveals that the anxiety and burden of secrecy in a teenager cause alienation, isolation, guilt, fear, depression, and an increase in family estrangement. In dissenting from invalidation of Minnesota's two-parent notice provision, Justice Anthony Kennedy agreed: "[T]o deny parents this knowledge is to risk, or perpetuate, estrangement or alienation from the child when she is in greatest need of parental guidance and support."

Supportive Parents

Critics also claim that parents will "beat, abuse, and even kill" their pregnant daughters, but there is no verifying evidence from states with such laws. Instead, there is substantial evidence that most parents support their daughter during an adolescent pregnancy. Worthington also found that after an initial period of disequilibrium, there emerges a more stable period of problem solving in which both mother and daughter take steps to resolve the pregnancy's difficulties.

In addition, a parental consultation statute usually contains a bypass permitting a doctor to proceed with abortion surgery *without* parental notice if the child is in an abusive home (including incest). Indeed, the abuse reporting requirement is an added safeguard for the minor to trigger remedial state intervention she otherwise may *not* have received in chronically abusive situations. As Justice Stevens wrote in 1981 in a concurring opinion for *H.L. v. Matheson:*

> A state legislature may rationally conclude that most parents will be primarily interested in the welfare of their children.... [A]n assumption that parental reaction will be hostile, disparaging or violent, no doubt persuades many children simply to bypass parental counsel which would in fact be loving, supportive and indeed, for some, indispensable.

Abortion tragedies rarely are reported honestly. Media attention instead focuses on the myth of abortion as the hallowed panacea for women. If the state legislatures explore the substantial evidence that has emerged, they will discover that the High Court's original concerns in *Bellotti* were right on target—and pass sensible laws restoring parental protection to pregnant minors in their time of critical need.

"Girls [are] dying from illegal or self-induced abortions—because they couldn't, or wouldn't, tell their parent(s) they were pregnant."

Parents Should Not Participate in Teenage Abortion Decisions

National Organization for Women

The National Organization for Women (NOW), the largest women's rights organization in the U.S., strongly supports women's right to legal abortion. In addition, NOW opposes parental consent laws, which require minors to notify at least one parent of, or obtain consent for, an intended abortion. In the following viewpoint, NOW maintains that such laws endanger the health and well-being of pregnant minors. For example, the organization contends that many minors are forced to seek illegal abortions because they fear having to tell their parents about their pregnancies. Also, NOW believes that delays in notifying parents will mean that abortions are performed later in the pregnancy when the risk of complications is higher. NOW's headquarters are in Washington, D.C.

As you read, consider the following questions:

1. Why are some minors reluctant to notify parents of their pregnancy, in NOW's opinion?
2. According to the authors, how can a minor living in a state with parental consent/notification laws get a legal abortion without notifying her parent(s)?

From "The Tragedy of Parental Involvement Laws," by the National Organization for Women, *National NOW Times*, January/February 1990. Reprinted by permission of *National NOW Times*.

Do parents want to know what is going on in their children's lives, especially if it involves serious problems? Sure they do.

In fact, this simple, and frankly simplistic, response is precisely the reason why parental consent and/or notification laws have taken hold in so many state legislative bodies across the country in the years since the *Roe v. Wade* Supreme Court decision legalizing abortion nationwide became the law of the land.

Since the *Roe* decision was handed down some 35 states have enacted laws requiring some form of parental involvement in the abortion decisions of their minor daughters, albeit with mixed results.

While some of these laws are not enforced because of various legal challenges, enough are enforced to affect the lives of thousands of teenage girls and to put many of their lives at risk.

That, in a nutshell, is what's wrong with these laws. Girls dying from illegal or self-induced abortions—because they couldn't, or wouldn't, tell their parent(s) they were pregnant.

The Myth of Family Protection

The most common argument heard in support of parental involvement in cases of minors' abortions is that parents have a "right" to know if a medical procedure is being performed on their children, since the parents are legally responsible for their children until they reach the age of majority at 18. Furthermore, the argument goes, parental consent is required by law for most medical procedures, such as appendectomies. So why should abortion be treated differently?

For the same reason that no one would argue that American society treats appendectomies and abortions the same way. The society, in fact, has treated matters of adolescent reproductive health differently for many years. For instance, the vast majority of states have laws that authorize minors to consent to treatment for venereal disease and even prenatal care without parental consent or notification. These laws were enacted in recognition of the fact that consent and notification laws hamper the willingness of minors to seek medical care for conditions affecting this area of their bodies and their lives.

Ironically, in many states these statutes rest side-by-side on the books with laws requiring parental consent and/or notification in matters of minors' abortions.

Even more ironic is that in a majority of states, once a minor has borne a child, she can consent to most, if not all, medical procedures for herself and her child. In other words, she must have her parents' consent or must notify them before obtaining an abortion. But once she's a mother herself, she gets control of her life in medical matters, and control of her child's life.

But legal rights and responsibilities aside, there are other compelling reasons why these laws are punitive and counterproductive and, instead of enhancing or protecting family relationships, in fact threaten just the opposite.

To begin with, there are the plain facts. Of the roughly 1.6 million legal abortions performed annually in this country, 12 percent or 192,000 are performed on minor girls. The majority of these girls, at least 55 percent, obtain abortions with their parents' knowledge—more often than not their parent(s) accompany them to the clinic or hospital. In the one percent of cases involving girls 15 or younger, the figure goes up to 75 percent of those who obtain abortions with their parents' knowledge.

All of which means that most teenage girls in America have the kind of family relationships that enable them to turn for help to those who care the most about them—their parents. And they don't need a law to compel them to do so.

Able to Decide on Their Own

Studies show that teenagers, like adults, can understand and reason about health care alternatives and make abortion decisions consistent with their own sense of what is right for them. Studies also note that adolescents are self-observant and able to provide their health histories as accurately as their parents.

American Civil Liberties Union, *Shattering the Dreams of Young Women,* 1991.

At the same time, there are a full 25 percent of minor girls who have reported in repeated studies that they have not, and would not, tell their parents about a pregnancy, regardless of any law. The most common reasons they give are as recognizable as the headlines seen daily in any newspaper in America: the likelihood of an abusive response from the parents, ranging from verbal or physical abuse to throwing them out of the house; anti-abortion or "sex is dirty" views of the parents; illness or substance abuse of the parents; or, in the case of 30 percent of girls 15 to 17 years old, they live with only one parent and rarely see the other one, if at all.

A Teen's Love Costs Her Life

In other words, many if not most of the teenagers who fall into this 25 percent come from dysfunctional family situations that no law passed anywhere by anybody can change, but which punitive laws can make worse by exposing young girls to abuse in order to punish them for being "bad." Not all of them, however, come from damaged family situations. There are some whose love and respect for their parents is so great, that they can't bear the thought of disappointing or hurting them. Such is the story of Becky Bell.

Becky Bell was a teenager in Indiana who died in 1988 at the age of 17. Because of that state's parental consent law, when she became pregnant Becky obviously could not receive a legal abortion in Indiana without first telling her parents and getting their permission. Unwilling to hurt the parents she loved with the news of her unintended pregnancy, according to her friends, she sought and obtained an illegal abortion. To this day Bill and Karen Bell don't know who performed the botched abortion on Becky, but they do know they lost her from a massive infection that set in as a result of the illegal abortion.

While their grief and their terrible sense of loss still hover over much of their daily lives, the Bells have dedicated themselves to speaking out against parental consent/notification laws because they "don't want to see happen to another girl what happened to Becky." As Karen Bell puts it, "you don't think it can happen to your family—until it does." Would Bill Bell trade his "parental right to consent" under Indiana law in order to have Becky back? Bill Bell will tell you he would trade anything to have Becky back.

Campaign to End Legal Abortion

It should be noted that parental consent/notification laws dealing with minors' abortions have never been initiated from the medical, professional, social services or advocacy groups who spend their time, talents and energy trying to help women, teenagers and their families.

These laws invariably have come from anti-abortion groups or legislators intent on making abortion illegal again in America. Period. These laws as well as others they have proposed or enacted, such as ending public funding for abortions for poor women, are seen as incremental gains in their agenda until they can stop legal abortions altogether.

The fact that much of the public has bought into the intended raw emotionalism of parental involvement in minors' abortion decisions is the result of a cynical, calculated campaign meant to distract the decidedly pro-abortion rights majority in this nation from the fundamental agenda of the anti-abortion camp which is an end to legalized abortion and, for many of them, most forms of birth control.

Unfortunately, the U.S. Supreme Court has upheld state parental consent/notification laws where these laws have provided an alternative to minors who are at risk if they involve their parents. The Court essentially has ruled that if an alternative is available for these teenagers to comply with consent/notification laws then their constitutional right to abortion guaranteed by the *Roe* decision is not violated.

The most common "alternative" found in these laws is called

the judicial bypass. This provision allows a pregnant minor to petition the courts for an exemption to the law and, if a judge determines that the petitioner is mature enough to make an abortion decision independent of her parents or that an abortion is in her best interests, then the judge can give the consent.

The hypocrisy and ludicrous nature of this procedure is self-evident. If a teenager is not mature enough to make a decision to abort an unintended and unwanted pregnancy, how in the world could the same teenager be mature enough to bear and raise a child?

Parental Involvement May Cause Abuse

In dysfunctional families (those with an alcoholic parent or a history of violence) or in families where there is already considerable stress (such as unemployment or a major illness), mandatory parental involvement is not only unlikely to result in more reasoned decisionmaking, it may lead instead to emotional and physical abuse as a result of the pregnancy disclosure.

Janet O'Keeffe and James M. Jones, *Issues in Science and Technology*, Fall 1990.

The anti-abortion camp's response to this, of course, is adoption. But in raising this so-called solution, they also conveniently ignore the fact that the public social services and foster care systems already are spilling over with children for whom adoptive homes can't be found.

Still, in fairness to the judges around the country who have been confronted with these cases, most have granted permission for most of the teenagers they have seen—even though some have behaved so bizarrely as to appoint an attorney to represent the fetus. The most common problem of this alternative is the thousands of teenagers the judges never do see.

The fact is, going to court for anything is an intimidating prospect for most people. Procedures for petitioning a court are beyond the knowledge of the average adult, much less a frightened, pregnant teenager. And finally getting to see a judge in light of the overload that jams most court dockets is an obstacle that can delay an abortion for weeks, not just days.

Given the fact that teenagers on average wait later into a pregnancy to seek an abortion than do older females, such delays can increase the medical risk of the abortion and, in too many cases, can result in the pregnancy being too advanced for a legal abortion unless there is a clear danger to the health or life of the teenager that mandates an affirmative decision.

The bottom line is that while the judicial bypass has been used successfully by a small number of pregnant minors, many more have fallen between the cracks of the system and have resorted to illegal options or have sacrificed their futures on the altar of compulsory motherhood.

Women who have abortions in America are predominantly young, single and of modest financial means. More than half, some 58 percent, are under the age of 25 and, as noted above, 12 percent are under the age of 18.

It is also important to note that although teenagers tend to wait longer to get abortions than older adults, nonetheless more than half of the abortions performed in this nation occur in the first eight weeks of pregnancy and 91 percent within the first 12 weeks of pregnancy, the first trimester. Only one-half of one percent occur after 20 weeks (mostly at 21 or 22 weeks), and only .01 percent (or 100 to 200 out of 1.6 million) are performed after 26 weeks, which the medical and scientific communities cite as roughly the point of fetal viability. These latter abortions can be performed legally only if the life of the woman or girl is in danger from continuing the pregnancy.

But what happens to girls under 18 who give birth—coerced or voluntarily? For starters, girls under 18 who give birth are only half as likely to graduate high school as those 20 years old or older. One survey conducted in Minnesota, a state with a parental notification law that is one of two such laws upheld by the Supreme Court in 1990, showed that a staggering 80 percent of mothers 17 years old or under never finish high school.

Teen Mothers and Poverty

Studies of the effects of teenage pregnancy and childbirth also show that families headed by teenage mothers are seven times more likely than others to be poor and to need some form of public assistance.

By contrast, women who delay childbirth until their 20s are four to five times more likely to finish college. In general, it can be said that the younger the mother at childbirth, the lower her family income.

There is also the issue of the health of children of teenage mothers. These children are twice as likely to die in infancy as those born to women in their 20s and even have a greater infant mortality rate than children born to women in their 40s, a high risk age group for pregnancy.

Much of this infant mortality is directly caused by low birth weight, a condition that also often leads to other problems, such as serious childhood illness and even birth injury and neurological defect, including mental retardation.

At the present time . . . more and more state legislatures are being pushed to enact parental consent/notification laws as a "compromise" on a highly volatile issue. And they are responding to this pressure with little knowledge or concern for the consequences of their actions.

"Abortion is far too important to be left to a woman and her doctor."

Men Should Take Part in the Abortion Decision

Bill Stout

While abortion is primarily thought of as a woman's issue, many men believe this perspective should change. In the following viewpoint, Bill Stout recounts the painful and traumatic experience of his wife's abortion, and concludes that men's feelings should be recognized and acknowledged in the abortion decision. Stout (1927–1989) was a nationally known CBS network correspondent for many years.

As you read, consider the following questions:

1. Why was his wife's decision to have an abortion so traumatic for the author?
2. Why was Stout confused by his wife's decision?

Bill Stout, "He (or She) Would Be 23," *The Human Life Review,* Summer 1976. Reprinted with permission.

Doctors and theologians are usually the only men who argue the abortion issue. Mostly, it's a women's debate. On one side: "We have the right to control our own bodies," and on the other: "It's a human life and killing it is wrong." That sort of thing.

But I had a jolt recently that sent me thinking seriously, *personally,* about abortion for the first time in more than 20 years. I suspect it was a shock that has hit a great many men, although few ever talk about it.

It came late on a Friday afternoon, at the start of a long holiday weekend. The freeways were jammed, of course, and when I started out for a business meeting on the far side of Los Angeles, the radio was full of "sigalerts." Since there was plenty of time, it seemed logical to skip the freeway mess and loaf across the city on the side streets. Easy enough, until even that oozing pace of traffic squeezed to a dead stop because of an accident at the corner of Beverly and Vermont. There my eye caught the window of a second floor office, and it hit me like a knee in the groin.

That office, in a building I hadn't even noticed in many years, was where I had taken my new bride for an abortion one blistering summer day in 1952. Suddenly I remembered . . . and I relived every detail.

We had been married two years and did not consider ourselves poor, but we were close. We had an old car, a few dollars in the bank, and I had a temporary job writing news stories for radio announcers. And she was pregnant.

Arguing for a Week

We had argued for more than a week after her first cautious announcement. I had adopted her young son by a previous marriage, but this would be our first baby together, and I was delighted. Minutes later I was appalled, then infuriated, by her insistence she would not go through with it. Even more hurtful, I suppose, in the callowness of that encounter so long ago, was that she had talked with several women friends before telling me anything. She already had the name of the doctor and was ready to make an appointment when I would be off from work to drive her to and from.

There was a lot of shouting and pleading that week and a good deal of pumping up (by me) of my prospects at the radio station. She pointed out that those were prospects only. She noted the sickly condition of our bankbook, plus the fact that we had 12 payments to go on our first television set. She also made the point hammered home today by the women's pro-abortion groups: it was, after all, *her* body, and the *decision* should be hers and hers alone.

That was the most painful week of our marriage, until the final anguish (of divorce) many years later. Of course, she got her way.

I dropped her at the curb outside the doctor's office then pulled around the corner to park and wait. It would be forty-five minutes, she said, no more than an hour at most. She had $200 in cash in her bag. No checks were accepted.

I spent the time multiplying and dividing. How much did this doctor *make* per hour? Per minute? How many of these jobs could he do in a day? Or in a year? Did he take just a two-week vacation so he could hurry back to the women with so many different reasons for ending pregnancies?

I remember his name. I can see the sign in his office window as clearly as if it were there now, just a few feet away. Seven letters, four in the first name; below them, centered on a separate line, "M.D." I never saw the man but I hated him then, and do to this moment, even though he died long ago.

Nothing to Talk About

When I saw her come out of his office, pale and wincing with each step, I leaped out of the car and ran to her. A couple of days later she was moving around with her usual energy and she made it clear that it was all over, with nothing to talk about. A year and a half later, with everything going fine for me in my work, she gave birth to our first baby, a normal healthy boy, and not long after that there came a daughter.

"I Want to Help Decide"

So far no one seems to have come up with any better alternative than simply making an abortion decision more palatable to a man. Some abortion counselors are trying harder than ever to encourage men to discuss their frustrations and to explore what the experience means to them.

The inadequacies of the approach are obvious. "I don't want someone to hold my hand and say they're sorry," said the man who stood silently by for his girlfriend's abortion. "I want to have a chance to help decide."

Patricia O'Brien, *St. Paul Pioneer Press*, October 13, 1983.

Yet, again and again, I have found myself wondering what that first one would have been like. A boy or a girl? Blonde or brunette? A problem or a delight? Whatever kind of person the lost one might have been, I feel even now that we had no right to take its life. Religion has nothing to do with that feeling. It was a "gut" response that overwhelmed me while stalled in the traffic that afternoon at Beverly and Vermont.

Now we were moving again. A few minutes later I was at my meeting in the Civic Center, in the office of an old friend, luckily, because by then I was in tears and they wouldn't stop. It wasn't easy but I finally told him how that glance at an office window had simply been too much for me, sweeping away a dam that had held for more than 20 years.

Haunting Feelings

If I am still wondering about the first one that never was, what about other men? How many of them share my haunted feeling about children who might have been? Why are we, the fathers who never were, so reluctant to talk about such feelings? And if it can be so painful for the men, how much worse must if be for the women who nurture and then give up the very fact of life itself?

Clearly, as the saying goes about wars and generals, abortion is far too important to be left to a woman and her doctor.

"Abortion is still a woman's right, a woman's choice. . . . When a man and a woman cannot come to agreement, it is the woman's wishes that must prevail."

A Man's Involvement Is of Secondary Importance

Kathleen McDonnell

Kathleen McDonnell has written extensively on women's health and other issues for a number of Canadian magazines. She also writes fiction and is the author of three plays. This viewpoint is excerpted from her book *Not an Easy Choice: A Feminist Re-Examines Abortion.* In it, McDonnell concedes that when possible, women should include the man in the abortion decision. However, when a man and a woman disagree over abortion, or when the woman decides she does not want to involve the man, the ultimate decision should be hers.

As you read, consider the following questions:

1. What is the most common male response to unwanted pregnancy, according to the author?
2. Why does McDonnell believe that men should be included in the abortion decision?
3. Under what circumstances, does the author argue, should men be excluded from the abortion decision?

Kathleen McDonnell, *Not an Easy Choice: A Feminist Re-Examines Abortion.* Boston: South End Press, 1984. Reprinted with permission of Women's Press, Toronto.

While some criticize feminists for ignoring the fetus in the abortion issue, others (often the same people) do so for ignoring men as well. And indeed, with our steady insistence that "abortion is a woman's right," we may sometimes forget, or appear to forget, that abortion always occurs in the context of sexual contact between a woman and a man. (Except, of course, in the rare case of an abortion where the pregnancy is the result of artificial insemination. Even then there is male involvement, but not *sexual* involvement.)

Often the man is no longer in the picture by the time the abortion takes place, or the woman has chosen not to tell the man that she is pregnant, or she may not even know for certain who the father is. But whether or not the man is present within the orbit of persons and events surrounding an abortion, the fact remains that men as a group are intimately and inextricably connected to abortion. Like making a baby, it takes two to create an unwanted pregnancy.

In dealing with abortion and other reproductive matters, feminists have gone a long way toward eradicating the sexist notion that unwanted pregnancy is the fault of the woman, a kind of punishment for sexual activity that men are not expected to share. But while fostering the notion that men should bear an equal share of responsibility in reproductive matters, feminists have been reluctant to accord them anything more than a minor role in reproductive decisions, especially where abortion is concerned. There are some perfectly good reasons for this. Women are the ones who bear children. Women are the ones, still, who are largely responsible for their care and nurturing. It is our bodies and our lives that are at issue, so the decisions must be ours as well. Besides, ample evidence over the centuries has shown us that we have been prudent not to accord men much say in reproductive matters, especially abortion, because on the whole they have not acquitted themselves well in this area.

Men and Abortion

The most common male response to unwanted pregnancy when it occurs outside of marriage has been to "take off," leaving the woman to bear the physical, the emotional and, often, the financial brunt of either having an abortion or carrying the pregnancy to term. Studies of abortion and its aftermath reveal that, more often than not, relationships do not survive an abortion: the majority of unmarried couples break up either before or soon after an abortion. In many cases, of course, the breakup is at the instigation of the woman, or the decision is a mutual one. But the most frequent scenario is that the man terminates the relationship on being told of the pregnancy, or shortly after the abortion, or he just gradually fades out of the picture. Male reluctance to accept responsibility in reproductive matters extends far beyond pregnancy and abortion, of course. The majority of men still regard the use of contraception as a woman's problem, for example. And men are increasingly disowning responsibility for their own biological children, as Barbara Ehrenreich demonstrates in her book *The Hearts of Men*. Over the past decade and a half men have begun to "take off" in unprecedented numbers, abandoning their traditional breadwinner roles, defaulting on support payments and leaving women to be the sole financial support of their children.

Male-dominated Society

I think I am only beginning to understand, as a man, why women are driven to the desperate violence of taking life in their wombs—in a society where men accept virtually no responsibility for their sexuality with women or for the personal care of their own children.

Jim Douglass, *Sojourners*, November 1980.

Often men take the opposite tack when confronted with an unplanned pregnancy: they stick around and demand that the woman not abort "their" child. This demand is rarely accompanied by an offer to raise and support the child, however. Personal accounts of abortion reveal this particular scenario with an astounding frequency: the man will say he is "against abortion" or forbid the woman to abort "his" child, without the slightest awareness of the responsibility that this position logically demands of him. A woman in one study even felt that her lover was "more logical and more correct" in his contention that "she should have the child and raise it without either his presence or his financial support." Another, a fifteen-year-old, acceded to her boyfriend's wish not to "murder his child." But after she decided against having an abortion, he left her to raise the child alone and "ruined my life," she said.

Proving Their Virility

This extraordinary attitude stems from a number of factors. First, there is the simple fact that, for many men, making a woman pregnant is a proof of virility, and they are unable to think beyond that to the consequences. One study of male and female attitudes toward childbearing showed that men tend to view it as a kind of testament to their "immortality," rather than in terms of a personal relationship with a particular child, as women tend to do. . . . Men are more likely to take "principled" stands on moral issues without any regard for the human circumstances. Simone de Beauvoir notes that

> men universally forbid abortion, but individually they accept
> it as a convenient solution of a problem; they are able to con-
> tradict themselves with careless cynicism. . . .

Though feminism has never actually worked out a position on the role of men in abortion, in practice we have designated only one appropriate role for them, that of the "supportive man." In this scenario the man is to provide emotional support to a woman facing an unwanted pregnancy, and to help her carry out her choice, whatever it may be. In fostering this role we may give men the message, intentionally or not, that they should put aside whatever feelings or preferences they might have and just "be there" for the woman. Some progressive, "feminist" men, who are sympathetic to the goals of the wom-en's movement and who in many cases actively work to support them, have particularly gravitated toward this role in their rela-tionships with women. (A lot of other men are, of course, not so cooperative!) So, to a large extent, what we have encouraged in men is a passive, auxiliary role in abortion, allowing them to participate in a way that is helpful, but perhaps not, in some im-portance sense, truly meaningful. Perhaps this is just what we want. Abortion is, after all, a woman's choice. . . .

We have to acknowledge . . . that there is a grave inconsistency between our eagerness to involve men in all other aspects of reproduction and our unwillingness to allow them a similar role in abortion. This means we must acknowledge and validate men's role in the act of procreation. It really does take two. This isn't to suggest that men's and women's parts in creating life are somehow equivalent, as some maintain. They obviously are not. Nature involves women in the reproductive process in a total physical and emotional way. We go through pregnancy, labour, birth, postpartum and breastfeeding, with all their attendant physical, hormonal and psychological changes. By contrast, na-ture does not even provide us with a sure way of verifying which man has fathered which child. But, if we are serious in our efforts to, in a sense, right nature's imbalance and make re-production a truly joint effort, it behooves us to make more room for men in the abortion process, to allow them a meaning-ful role that acknowledges their part in procreation.

A Minefield of Problems

This stance poses, of course, a veritable minefield of prob-lems, which we must traverse carefully if we are to maintain our hard-fought struggle for control over our bodies. The Right-to-Life movement has long argued for male involvement in abor-tion decisions—as long as the men involved are against abortion. On Father's Day, 1984, a group of anti-abortionists picketed a number of Toronto hospitals to dramatize their contention that men should have the right to veto abortions. Some of the participants interviewed used arguments that were uncomfortably close to the feminist view that reproduction should be a shared responsibility. Raising children "is not woman's work, it's humanity's work," said one man. We should have no illusions about the fact that our arguments for greater male involvement can and will be used against us. This does not mean that we should reject them altogether, but only that we must be continually clarifying and strengthening our position.

To many men, "meaningful involvement" equals control. The only power they know is power over others. They do not understand how to participate in truly cooperative decision-making. As a rule women are much more schooled in the art of cooperation, of sharing power and encouraging others to offer input, whether we agree with it or not. So when we call for greater male involvement in abortion and other reproductive matters, we must do so with the regrettable understanding that many men, perhaps most men, are not yet capable of this kind of power sharing, and we must act accordingly.

A Woman's Decision

We can say that we support male involvement in abortion decisions, but, as always, life presents us with complex, unwieldy situations where hard-and-fast rules can't be applied. For example, if the man withdraws from the relationship as soon as he finds out about the pregnancy, there is no question of his continued involvement in the process—he has made his choice. But what about women who don't tell their partners they are pregnant, who simply go off and quietly have an abortion? Are we dictating to them that they must involve their partners? Obviously we cannot do so. Most often when a woman does this, she has good reason to believe that telling her lover about the pregnancy may have bad repercussions. She may fear that he will try to prevent her from having the abortion, or may actually physically harm her. It is an uncomfortable fact that pregnancy is one of the situations in which wife battering is most likely to occur, and some men have been known to respond to the news of an unwanted pregnancy with rage and violence because they feel "tricked," or they blame the woman.

In the end we must come back to our starting point: abortion is still a woman's right, a woman's choice. This means that when push comes to shove, when a man and a woman cannot come to agreement, it is the woman's wishes that must prevail. We cannot allow men any kind of absolute veto over our abortion decisions.

Recognizing Statements That Are Provable

We are constantly confronted with statements and generalizations about social and moral problems. In order to think clearly about these problems, it is useful if one can make a basic distinction between statements for which evidence can be found and other statements which cannot be verified or proved because evidence is not available, or the issue is so controversial that it cannot be definitely proved.

Readers should be aware that magazines, newspapers, and other sources often contain statements of a controversial nature. The following activity is designed to allow experimentation with statements that are provable and those that are not.

The following statements are taken from the viewpoints in this chapter. Consider each statement carefully. *Mark P for any statement you believe is provable. Mark U for any statement you feel is unprovable because of the lack of evidence. Mark C for any statement you think too controversial to be proved to everyone's satisfaction.*

If you are doing this activity as a member of a class or group, compare your answers with those of other class or group members. Be able to defend your answers. You may discover that others will come to different conclusions than you do. Listening to the reasons others present for their answers may give you valuable insights into recognizing statements that are provable.

P = *provable*
U = *unprovable*
C = *too controversial*

1. Of the approximately 1.6 million abortions performed annually in the U.S., 12 percent are performed on minors.

2. Thirty-seven states have passed parental consent/notification laws.

3. Minors suffer from more anxiety, depression, and long-term guilt as a result of their abortions than do older women.

4. Parents are more likely to be supportive of a daughter when they are informed of her pregnancy than if they hear about it after the abortion.

5. The U.S. Supreme Court has upheld states' parental consent laws.

6. More than half of the abortions performed in the U.S. occur in the first eight weeks of pregnancy.

7. Families headed by teenage mothers are destined to live in poverty.

8. Most pregnant teenagers would rather keep their babies than have abortions.

9. Most Americans want abortion to be legal and safe.

10. Missouri is one of many states that restricts funding for most abortions.

11. Our culture devalues children before and after birth.

12. Fifty percent of all American teenagers are sexually active.

13. New York and California provide public funds for abortions.

14. There is no difference between a fetus and a baby.

15. A couple's sexual relationship never lasts after the woman has had an abortion.

16. In 1973, the U.S. Supreme Court made abortion on demand legal in the early stages of pregnancy.

17. State restrictions on abortion will not reduce the number of abortions.

18. Two-thirds of women who have had abortions believe minors should have parental permission for an abortion.

Periodical Bibliography

The following articles have been selected to supplement the diverse views presented in this chapter.

AUL Insights	"Restoring Parental Rights," November 1990. Available from Americans United for Life, 343 S. Dearborn St., Chicago, IL 60604.
Eleanor J. Bader	"Protecting Freedom of Choice," *The Humanist,* March/April 1990.
Christianity Today	"Father's Rights Case Declined by High Court," January 13, 1989.
Dena S. Davis	"Abortion and the Court: 'Undue Burden,' " *Christianity and Crisis,* November 26, 1990. Available from 537 W. 121st St., New York, NY 10027.
Sol Gordon	"Write On," *The Humanist,* September/ October 1990.
Sue Halpern	"The Fight over Teenage Abortion," *The New York Review of Books,* March 29, 1990.
John Leo	"The Moral Complexity of Choice," *U.S. News & World Report,* December 11, 1989.
Rita Moreno	"The Choice I Made," *Ms.,* January/ February 1991.
Peggy Orenstein	"Does Father Know Best?" *Vogue,* April 1989.
Eloise Salholz	"Teenagers and Abortion," *Newsweek,* January 8, 1990.
Rochelle Sharpe	"'She Died Because of a Law,'" *Ms.,* July/August 1990.
David Shribman	"Parental Notification and Consent Emerge as Key Abortion Issues," *The Wall Street Journal,* November 29, 1989.
Nan Underwood	"A Profound Choice," *Maclean's,* November 19, 1990.
Michael J. Weiss	"Equal Rights: Not for Women Only," *Glamour,* March 1989.
David Whitman	"When Pregnant Girls Face Mom and Dad," *U.S. News & World Report,* December 4, 1989.

Is Abortion
Immoral?

Abortion

Chapter Preface

For many people actively involved in the abortion debate, the most important issue is whether abortion is moral. Activists who oppose abortion believe it is the killing of an unborn child and can never be justified. They argue that to end the life of an unborn child is not only a great wrong, but also a threat to the sanctity of all life. As Pope John Paul II states, "If a person's right of life is violated at the moment in which he is first conceived in his mother's womb, an indirect blow is struck at the whole moral order."

Thus opponents of abortion believe the unborn child's right to life outweighs the woman's right to choose abortion. As author Vernie Dale writes, the pro-abortion groups "continue to urge women to climb toward what is viewed as their rights over the bodies of seventeen million aborted children."

Abortion rights activists vehemently disagree with these views. In fact, many believe that morality is irrelevant to the abortion decision. Abortion is not an agonizing moral dilemma, but simply a necessary and important right that all women must be allowed to exercise. Easy access to abortion improves women's quality of life, advocates believe, because women are not forced to bear and take care of children that they do not want or cannot afford to have. For pro-choice advocates, the right of women to have an abortion clearly and irrevocably must triumph over the rights of the unborn fetus. As authors Carole Dornblaser and Uta Landy write, "We know [abortion] can preserve relationships and families. We know it can enhance the quality of life. We know it can preserve life itself."

Finally, some people believe that both the pro-choice and antiabortion positions are lacking. For these people, placing abortion in the context of right and wrong lessens the ability for people to make thoughtful decisions about abortion. For these people, abortion is the taking of a human life, but sometimes this decision must and should be made. As Rachel Richardson Smith, a mother and theology student writes, "Why can we not view abortion as one of those anguished decisions in which human beings struggle to do the best they can in trying circumstances?"

Whether abortion is moral is a question that finds few people taking the middle ground. As readers examine the highly charged debates in this chapter, they ultimately must decide for themselves.

"Abortion is not merely the removal of some tissue from a woman's body. . . . Abortion is the destruction of an unborn baby."

Abortion Is Immoral

John O'Connor

For many people, the central issue in the abortion debate focuses on one question: Is abortion the taking of a human life? Many people who believe it is, including John O'Connor, the author of the following viewpoint, insist that abortion can never be a moral choice. O'Connor strongly denounces abortion as the killing of innocent children in their mothers' wombs, and urges that abortion be made illegal to stop this destruction of human life. O'Connor is the Roman Catholic archbishop of New York City and chairman of the Committee on Pro-Life Activities of the National Conference of Catholic Bishops.

As you read, consider the following questions:

1. How does O'Connor distinguish between the different types of people who believe abortion is acceptable?
2. Why does O'Connor believe that making abortion illegal will reduce the need for abortion?

John O'Connor, "Abortion: Questions and Answers," *Origins*, June 28, 1990, vol. 20, no. 7. Reprinted with permission.

Over the course of the years I have been asked many questions about life and abortion by many well-meaning people. Today I still find that many good people are confused. They really believe they are doing the right thing—or at least the best thing—when they support or encourage an abortion. Such is certainly the case with some parents who love a daughter and, as they put it, "don't want to see her life ruined by an unintended pregnancy." I believe the same is true of a number of social workers and other advisers of the young who believe that in promoting abortions they are performing a truly humane service to the mothers of the unborn, to unborn babies, whose lives they feel will not be happy (especially if they will be poor), and to society at large.

Anguished Parents

I received a letter recently, for example, from a set of anguished parents. Their talented young daughter is all set for college, but she has become pregnant. They tell me they are encouraging her to have an abortion because they don't want to see her career ruined. They say they are afraid abortion is a "sin," but that it would be a worse sin if their daughter couldn't go to college "just because she made a mistake and got pregnant." I know many people feel that way.

Then there are those who honestly believe it is only "fair" to permit pregnant girls or women to decide for themselves whether to carry or to abort a baby. They say: "A woman should have control over her own body. Nobody has the right to invade her privacy." They see free choice in all things as an essential characteristic of the American way of life, and regardless of how they themselves see abortion, they do not feel they have the right "to impose their beliefs on others."

There are at least three other kinds of people who consider abortion acceptable. There are those who believe that a baby in the womb is not really fully human, that only with birth does the baby achieve this status. Others believe that because the law permits abortion, it must be morally acceptable. Then there are those—and I believe they are many—who simply don't think about the subject at all. They don't see it as a serious issue. It has never personally touched their lives. Or perhaps they deliberately refuse to think about it because they would only become further confused.

While one finds a certain number of Catholics holding various of these positions, it's probably necessary to add another category altogether for those who argue that they are good Catholics but believe the church is wrong in its position on abortion or that the church has no right to "dictate" to them on this matter. I would distinguish this group from those Catholics who simply don't know or don't understand what the church teaches or why.

One can be compassionate and understanding about all these positions, but sadly nothing changes the objective reality: Abortion kills babies in their mothers' wombs. It pains me to say that, as I know it pains all people of good will, but it is the tragic reality. And there is another tragic reality that has nothing whatever to do with compassion, and that is that abortion is big business, netting hundreds of millions of dollars for abortionists.

I know that many are offended by the use of the word *killing*. Actually it is the word used in a famous editorial published in 1970 in the California Medical Association journal:

"Since the old ethic has not yet been fully displaced, it has been *necessary to separate the idea of abortion from the idea of killing, which continues to be socially abhorrent. The result has been a curious avoidance of the scientific fact which everyone really knows, that human life begins at conception and is continuous, whether intra- or extrauterine, until death.* The very considerable semantic gymnastics which are required to rationalize abortion as anything but taking a human life would be ludicrous if they were not often put forth under socially impeccable auspices. It is suggested that this schizophrenic sort of subterfuge is necessary because while a new ethic is being accepted the old one has not yet been rejected" (emphasis added) (from California Medicine, 113:67, 1970).

This editorial was not written to oppose abortion. It was simply an exceptionally frank warning to doctors that they had better adopt the new ethic and gear up for the brave new world of abortion ahead of them. As the editorial pointed out, some real twisting of words would be required to make people forget that abortion is the taking of human life. In other words, they would have to come up with another word for "killing," if they were ever to make abortion socially acceptable. But a change in words, unfortunately, does not change the reality. . . .

What Is Abortion?

It is my experience that there are a number of young people who undergo abortions and do not understand what is happening to them. As a matter of fact, doctors who perform abortions generally prevent the woman or girl from seeing what is happening, and pro-abortion organizations have consistently resisted any legislation which would require that a young girl be told what an abortion is or be required to wait even 24 hours before having an abortion.

The important thing perhaps is to emphasize what abortion is not. Abortion is not merely the removal of some tissue from a woman's body. Abortion is not the removal of a living "thing" that would become human if it were allowed to remain inside the woman's body. Abortion is the destruction of an unborn baby.

A new human life begins as soon as the egg has been fertilized. Science reveals without question that once the egg is fertilized every identifying characteristic of a brand-new human being is present, even the color of the eyes and the hair, the sex and everything else. Pregnancy is the period for this new human life to mature, not to "become human"—it already is. . . .

We Can Legislate Morality

Some people argue that changing laws will not eliminate abortions. It is certainly true that a change of heart is more important than a change of law. What is forgotten, however, is that the law is the great teacher. Children grow up believing that if a practice is legal, it must be moral. Adults who live in a society in which what was illegal and believed to be immoral is suddenly declared legal soon grow accustomed to the new law and take the "new morality" for granted. In fact, many people seem to fear that if they don't support the new law and the "new morality" it has introduced they will be considered undemocratic and "un-American."

It is amazing, for example, how smoking habits have been turned around. With the deluge of media advertising and the strict legal limitations put on smoking in places like New York City, many people now even feel embarrassed to smoke in public. Suddenly, with new laws in jurisdiction after jurisdiction, smoking is seen as less acceptable than ever before—actually immoral and irresponsible in the eyes of many. . . . There is no question: Law and changes in law constitute a mighty force if there is a determination to enforce it.

I have no doubt that a change in the law would go a long way toward changing the attitude of Americans toward the rights of the unborn, at least over the long haul. It is effective regarding virtually every other issue. For example, in 1966 at the White House Conference on Civil Rights, then-Solicitor General of the United States Thurgood Marshall (now a justice of the Supreme Court) had this to say about the effect a change in law can bring about:

"Of course law—whether embodied in acts of Congress or judicial decision—is, in some measure, a response to national opinion and, of course, non-legal, even illegal events, can significantly affect the development of the law. But I submit that the history of the Negro demonstrates the importance of getting rid of hostile laws and seeking the security of new friendly laws. . . .

"Provided there is a determination to enforce it, law can change things for the better. There's very little truth in the old refrain that one can not legislate equality. Laws not only provide concrete benefit, they can even change the hearts of men, some men anyway, for good or evil. . . . The simple fact is that most people will obey the law and some, at least, will be converted by it."

LANDMARK DECISION

ROE vs. WADE ABORTION RULING

LANDMARKS

Dick Wright. Reprinted by permission of UFS, Inc.

There are those who argue that we cannot legislate morality and that the answer to abortion does not lie in the law. The reality is that we do legislate behavior every day. Our entire society is structured by law. We legislate against going through red lights, smoking in airplanes and restaurants, selling heroin, committing murder, burning down people's homes, stealing, child abuse, slavery and a thousand other acts that would deprive other people of their rights. And this is precisely the key: Law is intended to protect us from one another regardless of private and personal moral or religious beliefs. The law does not ask me if I personally believe stealing to be moral or immoral. The law does not ask me if my religion encourages me to burn down homes. As far as the law is concerned, the distinction between private and public morality is quite clear. Basically, when I violate other people's rights I am involved in a matter of public morality, subject to penalty under law.

Is it outlandish to think that laws against abortion might have some protective effect? It is obvious that law is not the entire answer to abortion. Nor is it the entire answer to theft, arson, child abuse or shooting police officers. Everybody knows that. But who would suggest that we repeal the laws against such crimes because the laws are so often broken? . . .

Life Before Choice

No one has a right to choose to put an innocent human being to death. The use of ambiguous language and euphemisms has been tragically successful in switching the emphasis from "life" to "choice," so that those who are trying to defend life are accused of trying to deprive people of choice. The argument then becomes: "In a pluralistic society, what authority do you have to deprive me of my reproductive rights?" Reproductive rights, however, are not the issue; killing human beings is.

The church understands that there are circumstances in which some people believe that abortion is the lesser of evils. They believe, for example, that it would be better to have an abortion if a baby will be born retarded or deformed; or if a mother is poor or already has several children; or, as we noted above, if a young girl's education or career would be disrupted by a baby or her reputation damaged. . . .

The church recognizes that many hardships can occur with a pregnancy. But there is a fundamental principle which must always prevail: The end never justifies the means if the means are evil. In other words, no matter how difficult the alternatives, they cannot justify the direct killing of an innocent human being. What kind of world would it be if we were not faithful to that principle? Where would the killing stop?

Many people reject capital punishment. Yet before capital punishment is administered to someone who is charged with a heinous crime like murder, he or she is first tried by jury and found guilty. Yet many who reject capital punishment accept, support and consider it a "right" to take the life of an innocent unborn baby, who has never had a trial or been found guilty. To the church this is inconsistent.

American laws deny the right to kill innocent human beings or even various "endangered species" like certain fish, birds or animals. Why is it "un-American" to argue against the "right" to kill the unborn? The church mourns the ravages of the environment, pollution of the air, the rivers and lakes and oceans, the poisoning of wildlife, the potential of nuclear war and an accompanying holocaust. But sheer common sense, if not mercy for the helpless, demands that a society address before all else the destruction of its own children.

"The decision to have an abortion is made responsibly, in the context of a morally lived life, by a free and responsible moral agent."

Abortion Is Not Immoral

Mary Gordon

Mary Gordon, a novelist and short-story writer, is the author of *Final Payments, The Company of Women, Men and Angels, Temporary Shelter,* and *The Other Side.* In the following viewpoint, Gordon argues that abortion is not an immoral act, and that women who have abortions are neither immoral nor selfish. Because abortions usually take place when the embryo is merely a clump of cells and not a developed fetus, Gordon concludes that abortion is not immoral, and that a woman's life is more important than that of the embryo.

As you read, consider the following questions:

1. According to Gordon, how do pro-life activists view women who choose to have abortions?
2. How does the status of the fetus change as it develops over the course of a pregnancy, according to the author?

I am having lunch with six women. What is unusual is that four of them are in their seventies, two of them widowed, the other two living with husbands beside whom they've lived for decades. All of them have had children. Had they been men, they would have published books and hung their paintings on the walls of important galleries. But they are women of a certain generation, and their lives were shaped around their families and personal relations. They are women you go to for help and support. We begin talking about the latest legislative act that makes abortion more difficult for poor women to obtain. An extraordinary thing happens. Each of them talks about the illegal abortions she had during her young womanhood. Not one of them was spared the experience. Any of them could have died on the table of whatever person (not a doctor in any case) she was forced to approach, in secrecy and in terror, to end a pregnancy that she felt would blight her life.

I mention this incident for two reasons: first as a reminder that all kinds of women have always had abortions; second because it is essential that we remember that an abortion is performed on a living woman who has a life in which a terminated pregnancy is only a small part. Morally speaking, the decision to have an abortion doesn't take place in a vacuum. It is connected to other choices that a woman makes in the course of an adult life.

Moral Choices

Anti-choice propagandists paint pictures of women who choose to have abortions as types of moral callousness, selfishness, or irresponsibility. The woman choosing to abort is the dressed-for-success yuppie who gets rid of her baby so that she won't miss her Caribbean vacation or her chance for promotion. Or she is the feckless, promiscuous ghetto teenager who couldn't bring herself to just say no to sex. A third, purportedly kinder, gentler picture has recently begun to be drawn. The woman in the abortion clinic is there because she is misinformed about the nature of the world. She is having an abortion because society does not provide for mothers and their children, and she mistakenly thinks that another mouth to feed will be the ruin of her family, not understanding that the temporary truth of family unhappiness doesn't stack up beside the eternal verity that abortion is murder. Or she is the dupe of her husband or boyfriend, who talks her into having an abortion because a child will be a drag on his life-style. None of these pictures created by the anti-choice movement assumes that the decision to have an abortion is made responsibly, in the context of a morally lived life, by a free and responsible moral agent.

How would a woman who habitually makes choices in moral

terms come to the decision to have an abortion? The moral discussion of abortion centers on the issue of whether or not abortion is an act of murder. At first glance it would seem that the answer should follow directly upon two questions: Is the fetus human? and Is it alive? It would be absurd to deny that a fetus is alive or that it is human. What would our other options be—to say that it is inanimate or belongs to another species? But we habitually use the terms "human" and "live" to refer to parts of our body—"human hair," for example, or "live red-blood cells"—and we are clear in our understanding that the nature of these objects does not rank equally with an entire personal existence. It then seems important to consider whether the fetus, this alive human thing, is a *person*, to whom the term "murder" could sensibly be applied. How would anyone come to a decision about something so impalpable as personhood? Philosophers have struggled with the issue of personhood, but in language that is so abstract that it is unhelpful to ordinary people making decisions in the course of their lives. It might be more productive to begin thinking about the status of the fetus by examining the language and customs that surround it. This approach will encourage us to focus on the choosing, acting woman, rather than the act of abortion—as if the act were performed by abstract forces without bodies, histories, attachments.

This focus on the acting woman is useful because a pregnant woman has an identifiable, consistent ontology [existence], and a fetus takes on different ontological identities over time. But common sense, experience, and linguistic usage point clearly to the fact that we habitually consider, for example, a seven-week-old fetus to be different from a seven-month-old one. We can tell this by the way we respond to the involuntary loss of one as against the other. We have different language for the experience of the involuntary expulsion of the fetus from the womb depending upon the point of gestation at which the experience occurs. If it occurs early in the pregnancy, we call it a miscarriage; if late, we call it a stillbirth.

Reversal of Terms

We would have an extreme reaction to the reversal of those terms. If a woman referred to a miscarriage at seven weeks as a stillbirth, we would be alarmed. It would shock our sense of propriety; it would make us uneasy; we would find it disturbing, misplaced—as we do when a bag lady sits down in a restaurant and starts shouting, or an octogenarian arrives at our door in a sailor suit. In short, we would suspect that the speaker was mad. Similarly, if a doctor or a nurse referred to the loss of a seven-month-old fetus as a miscarriage, we would be shocked by that person's insensitivity: could she or he not understand that a fetus that age is not what it was months before?

Our ritual and religious practices underscore the fact that we make distinctions among fetuses. If a woman took the bloody matter—indistinguishable from a heavy period—of an early miscarriage and insisted upon putting it in a tiny coffin and marking its grave, we would have serious concerns about her mental health. By the same token, we would feel squeamish about flushing a seven-month-old fetus down the toilet—something we would quite normally do with an early miscarriage. There are no prayers for the matter of a miscarriage, nor do we feel there should be. Even a Catholic priest would not baptize the issue of an early miscarriage.

Crucial Distinctions

The difficulties stem, of course, from the odd situation of a fetus's ontology: a complicated, differentiated, and nuanced response is required when we are dealing with an entity that changes over time. Yet we are in the habit of making distinctions like this. At one point we know that a child is no longer a child but an adult. That this question is vexed and problematic is clear from our difficulty in determining who is a juvenile offender and who is an adult criminal and at what age sexual intercourse ceases to be known as statutory rape. So at what point, if any, do we on the pro-choice side say that the developing fetus is a person, with rights equal to its mother's?

The anti-choice people have one advantage over us; their monolithic position gives them unity on this question. For myself, I am made uneasy by third-trimester abortions, which take place when the fetus could live outside the mother's body, but I also know that these are extremely rare and often performed on very young girls who have had difficulty comprehending the realities of pregnancy. It seems to me that the question of late abortions should be decided case by case, and that fixation on this issue is a deflection from what is most important: keeping early abortions, which are in the majority by far, safe and legal. . . .

As a society, we are making decisions that pit the complicated future of a complex adult against the fate of a mass of cells lacking cortical development. The moral pressure should be on distinguishing the true from the false, the real suffering of living persons from our individual and often idiosyncratic dreams and fears. We must make decisions on abortion based on an understanding of how people really do live. We must be able to say that poverty is worse than not being poor, that having dignified and meaningful work is better than working in conditions of degradation, that raising a child one loves and has desired is better than raising a child in resentment and rage, that it is better for a twelve-year-old not to endure the trauma of having a child when she is herself a child.

When we put these ideas against the ideas of "child" or "baby," we seem to be making a horrifying choice of life-style over life. But in fact we are telling the truth of what it means to bear a child, and what the experience of abortion really is. . . .

It is essential for a moral decision about abortion to be made in an atmosphere of open, critical thinking. We on the pro-choice side must accept that there are indeed anti-choice activists who take their position in good faith. I believe, however, that they are people for whom childbirth is an emotionally overladen topic, people who are susceptible to unclear thinking because of their unrealistic hopes and fears. It is important for us in the pro-choice movement to be open in discussing those areas involving abortion which are nebulous and unclear. But we must not forget that there are some things that we know to be undeniably true. There are some undeniable bad consequences of a woman's being forced to bear a child against her will. First is the trauma of going through a pregnancy and giving birth to a child who is not desired, a trauma more long-lasting than that experienced by some (only some) women who experience an early abortion. The grief of giving up a child at its birth—and at nine months it is a child whom one has felt move inside one's body—is underestimated both by anti-choice partisans and by those for whom access to adoptable children is important. This grief should not be forced on any woman—or, indeed, encouraged by public policy.

A Moral Choice

In 1974, when I was 18, I had an abortion. I had become pregnant, as do untold numbers of teens, accidentally. I certainly wasn't looking to have an abortion, but neither did I have any moral qualms about it. Wanting or having a child was so out of the question that I did not wish to, nor felt I ought to be forced to, even entertain the idea. In my own personal and genuinely felt belief system, abortion was not in the least bit unethical: I didn't think then, and I don't now, that it was "murder" or "killing." . . . For me, abortion was and is a perfectly moral and valid decision—one that doesn't even have to be all that traumatic if people don't make it so.

Lynn Chancer, *The Village Voice*, April 11, 1989.

We must be realistic about the impact on society of millions of unwanted children in an overpopulated world. Most of the time, human beings have sex not because they want to make babies. Yet throughout history sex has resulted in unwanted pregnancies. And women have always aborted. One thing that is not hidden, mysterious, or debatable is that making abortion illegal will result in the deaths of women, as it has always done. Is our historical memory so short that none of us remember aunts, sisters, friends, or mothers who were killed or rendered sterile by septic abortions? Does no one in the anti-choice movement remember stories or actual experiences of midnight drives to filthy rooms from which aborted women were sent out, bleeding, to their fate? Can anyone genuinely say that it would be a moral good for us as a society to return to those conditions?

Thinking about abortion, then, forces us to take moral positions as adults who understand the complexities of the world and the realities of human suffering, to make decisions based on how people actually live and choose, and not on our fears, prejudices, and anxieties about sex and society, life and death.

"The Bible shows life begins at conception."

The Bible Prohibits Abortion

Paul B. Fowler

In the following viewpoint, Paul B. Fowler argues that the Bible prohibits abortion. Fowler maintains that Scripture teaches that life begins at conception, that unborn life is sacred, and that women who abort their children will be cursed by God. Fowler is pastor of St. Andrew's Presbyterian Church in America in Hollywood, Florida, and former professor of New Testament studies at Columbia Graduate School of Bible and Missions in Columbia, South Carolina.

As you read, consider the following questions:

1. How does Fowler use the account of the birth of Jesus to support the view that life begins at conception?
2. According to the author, in what way does Scripture show God relating to the fetus?
3. In the author's opinion, how does Scripture view the "untimely death" of the unborn?

Most evangelical Christians agree, at least on the surface, that abortion is wrong; few would put themselves entirely in the pro-choice camp by approving abortion-on-demand. But evangelicals still disagree about circumstances under which abortion is deemed justifiable or not justifiable.

If the Christian is to believe abortion is wrong, he should do so for sound biblical reasons. Nothing short of careful biblical analysis will do. Why then does such a variety of opinions exist among those who claim the Bible as their life guide? Not all are sure the Bible really speaks to the abortion question. Some believe the Bible is silent on the issue. Others find a few texts indirectly relevant but not clear enough to decide for or against abortion. When seeking to apply the biblical principles they do find relevant, such as those of the sanctity of human life and the need to act in love, they find the answers to the abortion question elusive.

Granted, the Bible is not a textbook on biology. But I do not think the Bible's stand on the abortion issue is as enigmatic as some might suppose. God's Word is still adequate to respond to the bioethical issues of our day, and especially to abortion. . . .

When Does Human Life Begin?

While pro-choice advocates try to make light of the significance of conception and deny it as the crucial moment that begins a human life, Scripture places a high importance on conception.

Of course, a major source for the idea of conception as the start of new life is the scriptural account of the birth of Jesus. The angel Gabriel, when explaining the process to the Virgin Mary, said: "'Behold, you will conceive in your womb, and bear a son, and you shall name Him Jesus'" (Luke 1:31). One can hardly speculate about Jesus' life, as to whether it began at the first heartbeat, quickening, viability, or birth. The angel messenger clearly announces the life of the Savior beginning with conception. Was there a period of time between conception and when he became a *person*? I think not! . . .

We might ask, Did the biblical writers and the people living then really understand conception that clearly? After all, it has only been since the early nineteenth century that science has discovered what takes place biologically during conception. Moreover, the Bible is not a textbook on biology. What did the ancients understand about conception?

Obviously, people in biblical times did not have the benefit of modern biology. But they did have a basic understanding of the processes of conception and pregnancy as well as birth. The prophetic curse on Ephraim follows the process of life back to its origin:

> As for Ephraim, their glory will fly away like a bird—
> No *birth*, no *pregnancy*, and no *conception*! (Hosea 9:11)

Some forty times Scripture refers to conception as the start of new life in the womb of the mother. In the Genesis narratives alone, the phrase "conceived and bore" is found eleven times. The close pairing of the two words clearly emphasizes conception, not birth, as the starting point of life. . . .

The biblical writers never say the words, "Life begins at conception." But they consistently refer to conception as the starting point of a person's life, or metaphorically of the life of an idea. The usage is consistent throughout Scripture, even with its many writers extending over a period of some fifteen hundred years. . . .

Created in God's Image

Abortion is wrong. Both the Bible and biology point away from the modern notion that the fetus is merely a physical appendage of the mother rather than an independent human being. We must act on the belief that from the moment of conception, we are dealing with a human being created in the image of God. We must stop aborting millions of unborn babies each year.

Ronald J. Sider, *Christianity Today*, 1989.

That the Bible shows life begins at conception raises an even more important issue: What value does Scripture place upon human life once it has been conceived? Certainly it is a high value—but how high? The value of the unborn in Scripture may be studied in several ways: by their relation to the image of God, by their relation to God, by their continuity with postnatal life, and by the views about their untimely death.

Relation to the Image of God

Several verses assume explicitly or implicitly that the fetus is made in God's image. Genesis 5:3 reads: "When Adam had lived one hundred and thirty years, he became the father of a son in his own likeness, according to his image, and named him Seth." Most commentators interpret the phrases, "in his own likeness, according to his image," as meaning the image of God. The Hebrew verb *Yalad*, rendered here "became the father of," is often translated "begot." The verb's primary meaning is "to bear" or "to bring forth children." However, verbs have different forms in Hebrew, and the verbal form in this verse is the causal form. We could translate it literally, Adam "caused to bring forth" Seth, the cause being sexual intercourse and the resulting conception.

If this translation is correct, then Adam and Eve were the only ones literally created in God's image. Seth (and all other descendants of Adam and Eve) received the image of God through procreation. Seth's essential humanness was already present at conception.

The presence of the image of God may also be assumed when the Bible refers to the sinful nature of the unborn. For if the unborn can be shown to have a moral nature, would this not be evidence in favor of their being in the image of God? The verse most often recited in this regard is Psalm 51:5. In repentance over his sin with Bathsheba, David laments:

> Behold, I was brought forth in iniquity,
> And in sin did my mother conceive me.

This certainly supports the notion that man already bears God's image marred by sin—from conception on. . . .

We may conclude that man's moral, spiritual faculty is already present in the fetus before birth. If the image of God pertains to man's moral nature, then that nature has been passed on from Adam (Genesis 5:3). It is hard to argue that someone is not a person who has moral attributes. . . .

Relationship with God

The relationship of God to the fetus is significant. As Harold O.J. Brown explains:

> If God relates in a personal way to a human creature, this is evidence that that creature is made in God's image. And it is abundantly evident from Scripture that God relates to us and is personally concerned for us before birth.

Scripture shows God relating to the fetus in several intimate ways. First, a number of references concur that God oversees the development of the fetus. Job teaches (31:13-15) that God not only made him in the womb, but also fashioned everyone, including Job's slaves. The psalmist acknowledges: "Thy hands made me and fashioned me" (119:73). David reflects on the amazing way God "knit" his body "in the secret place" (Psalm 139:13-16). Jeremiah reports what the Lord had said to him:

> Before I formed you in the womb I knew you,
> And before you were born I consecrated you (1:5)

A second way God relates personally to the unborn is preparing them as individuals for a specific calling. Jacob was given preeminence over Esau, though "not yet born" (Romans 9:11). Samson's mother was told not to eat anything unclean nor to drink wine or strong drink while pregnant, "'for the boy shall be a Nazirite to God from the womb; and he shall begin to deliver Israel from the hands of the Philistines'" (Judges 13:3-5). God knew Jeremiah even before he was conceived and consecrated him while in the womb (Jeremiah 1:5). Paul writes that God had set him apart, even "from my mother's womb" (Galatians 1:15). Other examples could be cited. Clearly, life in the womb is a stage in the realization of God's plan for an individual.

God's concern and active involvement in the progress of the unborn differs strongly from the pro-abortionist's dismissal of the unborn as worthless nonpersons. John Davis summarizes the Bible passages well when he writes:

> All these texts indicate that God's special dealings with human beings can long precede their awareness of a personal relationship with God. God deals with human beings in an intensely personal way long before society is accustomed to treat them as persons in the "whole sense.". . . God's actions present a striking contrast to current notions of personhood.

God's personal involvement with the unborn provides the foundation for their personal worth. If we are persons because God has related to us in a personal way, then the unborn are also persons since God's care for them obviously begins in the womb.

Psalm 139:13-16

For Thou didst form my inward parts;
Thou didst weave me in my mother's womb
I will give thanks to Thee, for I am fearfully and
    wonderfully made;
Wonderful are Thy works,
And my soul knows it very well.
My frame was not hidden from Thee,
When I was made in secret,
And skillfully wrought in the depths of the earth.
Thine eyes have seen my unformed substance;
And in Thy book they were all written,
The days that were ordained for me,
When as yet there was not one of them.

The Bible, The Psalms

A third way Scripture indicates the fetus's value is that a significant continuity between prenatal and postnatal human life is assumed. David sees *himself* as having existed in his mother's womb (Psalm 139:13ff.). The nativity narratives concerning John the Baptist and Jesus unmistakably point to a continuity between pre- and postbirth. Every time we read passages such as Genesis 21:2-3—"So Sarah conceived and bore a son to Abraham. . . . And Abraham called the name of his son who was born to him . . . Isaac"—a personal continuity is assumed from conception through birth to a named individual.

The biblical writers did not use different words to label prenatal and postnatal life. The same Hebrew and Greek terms are often used to refer both to the born and the unborn. For example, *Geber* is a Hebrew noun usually translated man, male, or husband. In Job 3:3, Job curses the night in which it was said, "a man-child [*geber*] is conceived." *Yeled* is a term in Hebrew commonly translated child or boy. Yet Genesis 25:22 refers to *yeladim* (children) struggling inside the womb of Rebekah. Moses recites a law in which a *Yeled* (child, boy) comes forth from a woman (born prematurely). . . .

The Bible commonly applies personal language to the unborn. Hosea comments on how, in the womb, Jacob took "his brother" by the heel (12:3). The personal pronouns *me*, *my*, and *I* are regularly used by writers referring to their lives before birth. Some scholars claim this does not mean much since most people use personal pronouns as a normal way of speaking. However, this manner of speaking of life in utero at the very least warns us against making a sharp separation between the pre- and postnatal periods in our lives for the purpose of demeaning the value of the unborn.

Their Untimely Death

A fourth, though negative, way of ascertaining the value of the unborn is to look at Scripture's view of their "untimely death." We have seen how conception and birth were viewed as wonderful blessings from the Lord. The opposite was also true; miscarriages and murders of the unborn (pregnant women being ripped open) were viewed as a dreadful curse for any people. These themes are highly visible throughout Scripture.

Hazael, future king of Aram, asked Elisha why he wept for him. Elisha replied: "'Because I know the evil that you will do to the sons of Israel: their strongholds you will set on fire, and their young men you will kill with the sword, and their little ones you will dash in pieces, and their women with child you will rip up'" (2 Kings 8:12). It was Amos who prophesied against the sons of Ammon that they would surely be punished "because they ripped open the pregnant women of Gilead/ In order to enlarge their borders" (Amos 1:13). The "ripping open of pregnant women" killed both child and mother.

The untimely death of the unborn or newly born is often recalled to picture the curse of God upon a people due to their unrighteousness. In a gruesome prophecy, Hosea declared that due to Israel's sins, God would close the nation's wombs. Then he continued:

> Give them, O Lord—what wilt Thou give?
> Give them a miscarrying womb and dry breasts.
>
> Ephraim is stricken, their root is dried up,

They will bear no fruit.
Even though they bear children,
I will slay the precious ones of their womb.

Samaria will be held guilty,
For she has rebelled against her God.
They will fall by the sword,
Their little ones will be dashed in pieces,
And their pregnant women will be ripped open.

(Hosea 9:14, 16; 13:16).

Because these passages refer to miscarriages and the ripping open of pregnant women as the ultimate form of punishment for sin and as a sign of a dreadful curse, it is not difficult to see why abortion was so alien to the Hebrew mind. In their world and life view, there was no place for abortion or the destruction of life in the womb. No doubt this is why abortion is not discussed in Scripture. There was no need for a prohibition against feticide any more than against uxoricide (wife-killing); both were covered by the sixth commandment against homicide, "You shall not murder" (Exodus 20:13).

When we apply these texts to our times, it is clear that it is quite a responsibility to make a decision to abort one's own child. Such an action deliberately brings on one's own family the fate which in Scripture is the symbol of divine curse! Conversely, the decision to care for the "precious ones" of the womb (Hosea 9:16) is in character with the purposes and desires of God. . . .

Scripture Is Clear

We may have been prone to think Scripture could not answer the moral issues of our day. Yet God's Word is still sufficient to respond adequately even to the issue of abortion. We find that the entire ethos and underlying assumptions and themes of Scripture provide a thorough and clear response to abortion.

"There is no condemnation or prohibition of abortion anywhere in the Bible."

The Bible Does Not Prohibit Abortion

John M. Swomley

The United Methodist church supports a woman's right to abortion, although it believes that abortion should not be used as a method of birth control, for sex selection, or genetic engineering. In the following viewpoint, John M. Swomley, a well-known United Methodist social commentator, presents a religious defense of abortion. Swomley contends not only that the Bible does not condemn abortion, but that it clearly states that human life begins at birth. Accordingly, because the fetus is at most a potential human being, the practice of abortion is morally acceptable. Swomley is also a professor emeritus of social ethics at the St. Paul School of Theology in Kansas City, Missouri.

As you read, consider the following questions:

1. In which passages does the Bible deal with the subject of abortion, according to the author?
2. What right does a woman have to an abortion, in Swomley's opinion?
3. In what ways does Swomley criticize the position of the Roman Catholic church on abortion?

John M. Swomley, "Human Beings: In God's Image," *Christian Social Action*, April 1990. Reprinted with permission.

The tragedy of an unwanted pregnancy that threatens a woman's life or health existed in the ancient world, as it does today. At the time the Bible was written, abortion was widely practiced in spite of heavy penalties. The Assyrian code prohibited abortion with this statement: "Any woman who causes to fall what her womb holds . . . shall be tried, convicted and impaled upon a stake and shall not be buried." In Assyria the fetus was given more value than the woman.

Although the Hebrews were influenced by many of the laws of their Assyrian, Sumerian and Babylonian neighbors, all of which forbade abortion, the Hebrew scriptures had no laws forbidding abortion. This was chiefly because of the higher value placed upon women. There are, however, some references to the termination of pregnancy. In Exodus 21:22-25 a pregnant woman has a miscarriage as a result of a fight between two men. The penalty for the loss of the fetus was a fine; if the woman was killed, the penalty was "life for life." It is obvious from this passage that the men who terminated the woman's pregnancy are not regarded as murderers unless they killed the woman. The woman, undeniably, had greater moral and religious worth than the fetus.

There is also reference in the Mosaic law to "abortion on request" (Numbers 5:11-31) if a husband suspects his wife is pregnant by another man. The "husband shall bring his wife to the priest" who shall mix a drink that was intended to make her confess or be threatened with a miscarriage if she had been unfaithful to her husband.

No Biblical Condemnation

Aside from these passages, the Bible does not deal with the subject of abortion. Although both Testaments generally criticize the practices of their neighbors, such as idol worship and prostitution, as well as various immoral acts in their own land, there is no condemnation or prohibition of abortion anywhere in the Bible in spite of the fact that techniques for inducing abortion had been developed and widely used by the time of the New Testament.

A key question in the abortion controversy is, "When does human life begin?" The Bible's clear answer is that human life begins at birth with breathing. In Genesis 2, God "breathed into his nostrils the breath of life and man became a living being" (in some translations, "a living soul"). The Hebrew word for a human being or living person is *nephesh*, the word for breathing. "Nephesh" occurs hundreds of times in the Bible as the identifying factor in human life. This is consistent with modern medical science, as a group of 167 distinguished scientists and physicians told the Supreme Court in 1989 that "the most important

113

determinant of viability is lung development," and "viability has not advanced to a point significantly earlier than 24 weeks of gestation" because critical organs, "particularly the lungs and kidneys, do not mature before that time."

God's Grace and the Abortion Decision

Contemporary Christians will do well to follow the biblical pattern in treating the subject of elective abortion. The claim that the Bible teaches that the fetus is a person from the moment of conception is problematic at best. Such a judgment rests on subjective and personal factors, not explicit biblical teachings. The Bible's portrait of person centers on the woman and the man who unquestionably bear the image of God and live in responsible relation to him. . . .

God's grace is extended to those who accept the responsibilities of parenthood to make difficult choices in the midst of the moral ambiguity of tragic and perplexing circumstances.

Paul D. Simmons, *Abortion Rights and Fetal "Personhood,"* 1989.

In the Christian scriptures, the Incarnation, or "the Word made Flesh" was celebrated at Jesus' birth, not at a speculative time of conception. The biblical tradition is followed today by counting age from the date of birth rather than from conception, a date people do not know or seek to estimate. The state issues no conception certificates, only birth certificates.

The Vatican assumption that human life begins at conception is derived from Greek philosophy, rather than the Bible, and implies that a human being is created at a specific moment instead of by a process that takes about nine months. To focus on the biological realities of genes and chromosomes present at conception or to think of personhood solely in materialist or biological terms neglects the spiritual nature and characteristics of humans, which the Bible describes as created "in the image of God" (Genesis 1:26-27). This does not refer to biological similarities but to the abilities to love and to reason, self awareness, transcendence, and freedom to choose, rather than to live by instinct.

The brain is crucial to such human abilities. The 167 scientists mentioned above said, "It is not until sometime after 28 weeks of gestation that the fetal brain has the capacity to carry on the same range of neurological activity as the brain in a full-term newborn."

Fifty-one percent of all abortions in the United States occur before the eighth week of pregnancy; more than 91 percent by the 12th week, in the first trimester; and more than 99 percent by 20 weeks, which is about four weeks before the time of viability when 10 to 15 percent of fetuses can be saved by intensive care. This means that in the "tragic conflict of life with life that may justify abortion" (from the United Methodist Social Principles) there is no brain or neo-cortex, and hence no pain in cases of early abortion.

Every termination of potential human life is a normal problem to be justified only because of the "damage [that] may result from an unacceptable pregnancy" (United Methodist statement). Contrary to the statement, abortion is rarely used as a method of birth control, and, according to the Guttmacher Institute, is so seldom used as a means of gender selection, except for a few Mideastern couples, that no data are available.

An Extreme Measure

Abortion is viewed by most women as an extreme measure to be considered only when there is no other reasonable alternative. Those who claim abortion is a method of birth control refer to the fact that some birth control devices function immediately after conception to prevent implantation. The argument that conception is more crucial to the birth process than implantation is irrelevant, as both are necessary steps before the formation of individual biological life can begin.

Up to 50 percent of fertilized eggs do not implant. Of those that do, between 20 percent and 50 percent miscarry. Of all implantations, only about 10 percent are successful pregnancies. If there is objection to the prevention of implantation as a method of abortion, on the assumption that this is the taking of life, then nature or God is the greatest killer, because there are more spontaneous preventions of implantation than those performed medically. In other words, God does not will that every conception should eventuate either in implantation or in birth. This is consistent with our previous assertion that a fetus, as well as a fertilized egg, is a potential rather than an actual human being.

Actually, those who speak of a human being as present at conception are guilty of "prolepsis," a propaganda term which *Webster's Dictionary* defines as "an anticipating, especially the describing of an event as if it had already happened." This is what happens when the few cells after conception or a fetus in the early trimesters are spoken of as a baby or an unborn child.

Some years ago at a meeting of the American Society of Christian Ethics, we were confronted with a case of a three-year-old child and an 18-week fetus, each with a dread disease for which there was only one injection of medicine in Chicago, whose airports had been shut down by a blizzard. We unanimously concluded that the three-year-old child should get the injection. The moral difference is that the child is among us in a way that the fetus is not. It is a claim based on relationship, rather than a legal point of birth.

A further illustration comes from Roman Catholic doctrine. Although the Roman Catholic hierarchy strongly opposes intentional abortion, in practice it sometimes recognizes the priority of the woman over the fetus, as evident in the following from a US Catholic Conference publication:

"Operations, treatments and medications, which do not directly intend termination of pregnancy, but which have as their purpose the cure of a proportionately serious pathological condition of the mother are permitted when they cannot be safely postponed until the fetus is viable, even though they may or will result in the death of the fetus.". . .

Rights of Living Persons/Potential Persons

What right does a woman have to an abortion? One answer is that the rights of living persons take precedence over any rights of potential persons, just as immediate or present needs take precedence over probable future or potential needs. This question can also be stated as: What right does anyone have to impose mandatory pregnancy on a woman? The ethical question is not whether abortion can be justified but whether we focus on an embryo or fetus as the object of value or whether we focus on the woman as a moral agent who must have freedom of choice.

When Moses asked God His name, God said, "I am who I am," or, in the future tense, "I will be who I will be." God is a free moral being, not determined by cause and effect. Humans made in the image of God are likewise moral beings precisely because they engage in free choice in all of their decisions.

A passage in Genesis describes humans as moral decision-makers who, like God, know the difference between good and evil. Of all the animals in the Garden of Eden only one, the human person, was free to make choices, with the ability to choose between good and evil and, of course, to face the consequences of that choice.

In the New Testament, there is an emphasis on the priesthood of all believers: "You are a chosen race, a royal priesthood, a holy nation, God's own people" (I Peter 2:9). Each believer has direct access to God and has the ability to know and do God's revealed will. We are not bound by any natural law derived from Greek philosophy; neither are we bound by the ancient Jewish law or by any other legalism handed down by any religious or spiritual leader.

When Jesus said, "Man was not made for the Sabbath; the Sabbath was made for man," he struck at the heart of legalism or rules for their own sake. The Bible tells us that we live by grace. This means that God acts within human beings to set us free and to enable us to assume responsibility for ourselves, our environment, and our future. If we make wrong choices, God's grace is available as judgment and forgiveness.

Abortion and the Kingdom of God

I believe that as Christians, we are called to usher in the kingdom of God. . . . Life for a Christian is more than breathing in and out. Until people have a home in which to raise their children, the safety and security of whatever they need to do that well, then abortion needs to be a choice. Clearly, giving a woman the right to abortion is a compassionate stand, and anytime compassion rules over judgment, we see the kingdom of God.

Christine Grimbol, *The Choices We Made*, 1991.

Humans, by the grace of God, have developed medicine, surgery and psychiatry to prolong and enhance life. These same medical approaches can be chosen to prolong or enhance the life of a woman for whom a specific birth would be dangerous.

Integrity and Welfare of Women

Another comparatively recent emphasis in theological ethics is concerned with the integrity and welfare of women. Women, whose lives and freedom have been largely at the mercy of men for centuries, must make or be involved in decisions that affect their lives, their futures, their families. To refuse on principle to permit a woman to consider her life or welfare when it seems threatened by pregnancy is to say that only men are the recipients of God's grace in terms of freedom and responsibility. It is also to say that the primacy of the right to bodily life of the fetus places all other considerations, including the health, worth and dignity of women, on a lower level.

Thus far I have contrasted Catholic and Protestant doctrine at two basic points. One is the issue of legalism. Must all of us obey the rules formulated by the Pope or are Protestants still free by grace and justified by faith? Given these differences about legalism, the phrase "sacredness of life" means one thing to Catholic bishops—that the life of the fetus is all-important. But to most Protestants and many others it means that there is a presumptive right to life which is not absolute but conditioned by the claims of others. For us the right to life and the sacredness of life mean that there should be no absolute or unbreakable rules which take precedence over the lives of existing human persons.

The pro-life position is really a pro-fetus position and the pro-choice position is really pro-woman. Those who take the pro-fetus position define the woman in relation to the fetus. They assert the rights of the fetus over the right of a woman to be a moral agent or decision maker with respect to her life, health, and family security.

Controlling Procreation: Women or Church?

The second doctrinal issue in both the abortion and the birth control controversy is who is to have the power to control procreation: women in consultation with their partners and their physicians, or the church. The historic natural law position of the Catholic church was not concerned about feticide, but about the sin of sexuality if it interfered with procreation as contraception and abortion do. Since the Pope and the bishops have been unable to persuade women to accept control by the church over their sexuality, their only hope for reasserting that control is to persuade the state through political power to make a church sin into a crime affecting all women. The low view of women, which keeps them from being ordained and insists that their proper role is that of mother, is not simply Catholic theology but fundamentalist political ideology, which is also anti-woman. The key phrase is not simply "pro-life," but "pro-family," which is always defined as a patriarchal family. . . .

Is there a right to life in law or in biblical faith? In answering this question, we must distinguish between a virtue—doing something we ought to do—and a right. If I am walking along the bank of a river or lake and someone who cannot swim falls or jumps in, we could argue that I ought also to jump in, to rescue the drowning person, even if my own life is at stake. But the person who jumps or falls in cannot claim that I *must* jump in because he/she has a right to life. The mere fact that I *ought* to rescue another does not give that other person a right against me.

The common law rule is that we have no duty to save the life of another person unless we voluntarily undertake such an obligation as a lifeguard does in contracting to save lives at a swimming pool. Neither is there a biblical mandate that each of us is morally required to risk our lives to save the life of another. Jesus treated as highly exceptional and an evidence of great love the act of a person who "lay down his life for his friends" (John 15:13). . . .

No woman should be required to give up her life or health or family security to save the life of a fetus that is threatening her well-being. At the very least she is entitled to self-defense. On the other hand, many women are willing to sacrifice their health and future in order to have one or more children. The religious community that respects the autonomy of women must respect equally their freedom of choice.

118

a critical thinking activity

Distinguishing Between Fact and Opinion

This activity is designed to help develop the basic reading and thinking skill of distinguishing between fact and opinion. Consider the following statement: "Most abortions take place within the first twelve weeks of pregnancy." This is a factual statement because it could be checked by looking up government health statistics which record this type of information. But the statement "The stage in pregnancy when abortion takes place is unimportant because abortion is murder whenever it occurs" is an opinion. Many people may not believe that abortion is murder.

When investigating controversial issues it is important that one be able to distinguish between statements of fact and statements of opinion. It is also important to recognize that not all statements of fact are true. They may appear to be true, but some are based on inaccurate or false information. For this activity, however, we are concerned with understanding the difference between those statements which appear to be factual and those which appear to be based primarily on opinion.

Most of the following statements are taken from the viewpoints in this chapter. Consider each statement carefully. *Mark O for any statement you believe is an opinion or interpretation of facts. Mark F for any statement you believe is a fact. Mark I for any statement you believe is impossible to judge.*

If you are doing this activity as a member of a class or group, compare your answers with those of other class or group members. Be able to defend your answers. You may discover that others come to different conclusions than you do. Listening to the reasons others present for their answers may give you valuable insights into distinguishing between fact and opinion.

> O = *opinion*
> F = *fact*
> I = *impossible to judge*

1. Abortion is the destruction of an unborn baby.
2. Some people argue that changing laws will not eliminate abortions.
3. *Roe v. Wade* should be overturned.
4. American laws deny the right to kill human beings or even certain endangered species of fish, birds, or animals.
5. A new human life begins as soon as the egg has been fertilized.
6. Most women and girls who undergo abortions do not understand what is happening to them.
7. Women from all economic levels have had abortions.
8. The decision to have an abortion is made responsibly, in the context of a morally lived life, by free and responsible women.
9. A seven-week-old fetus is different from a seven-month-old one.
10. Sex sometimes results in unwanted pregnancy.
11. Third-trimester abortions are extremely rare.
12. Making abortion illegal will result in the deaths of women.
13. Scripture refers to conception as the start of new life at least forty times.
14. God's concern for the unborn differs strongly from the proabortionist's dismissal of the unborn as worthless nonpersons.
15. Both the Bible and biology disprove the modern notion that the fetus is not an independent human being.
16. A key question in the abortion controversy is, When does human life begin?
17. To abort one's own child brings on a curse from God.
18. Up to 50 percent of fertilized eggs do not implant.
19. No woman should be required to give up her life or health or family security to save the life of a fetus that is threatening her well-being.
20. Abortion is viewed by most women as an extreme measure to be considered only when there is no other reasonable alternative.

Periodical Bibliography

The following articles have been selected to supplement the diverse views presented in this chapter.

David Earle Anderson
"Abortion and the Churches," *Christianity and Crisis*, March 4, 1991. Available from 537 W. 121 St., New York, NY 10027.

Daniel Callahan
"An Ethical Challenge to Prochoice Advocates," *Commonweal*, November 23, 1990.

Judith Craig
"A Bishop's Letter to Her Goddaughter," *Christian Social Action*, April 1990. Available from 100 Maryland Ave. NE, Washington, DC 20002.

Jason DeParle
"Beyond the Legal Right: Why Liberals and Feminists Don't Like to Talk About the Morality of Abortion," *The Washington Monthly*, April 1989.

Mark Ellingsen
"The Church and Abortion: Signs of Consensus," *The Christian Century*, January 3-10, 1990.

John Elson
"Bishops, Politicians and the Abortion Crisis," *Time*, February 19, 1990.

Kenneth Guentert and Jo McGowan
"Is There Room for Discussion in the Abortion Debate?" *U.S. Catholic*, April 1991.

Nat Hentoff
"You Don't Have to Believe in God to Be Prolife," *U.S. Catholic*, March 1989.

Frances Kissling
"Ending the Abortion War: A Modest Proposal," *The Christian Century*, February 21, 1990.

National Review
"Abortion: The Debate, the Politics, the Morality," December 22, 1989.

Anna Quindlen
"The Abortion Account," *The New York Times*, April 8, 1990.

Ronald J. Sider
"Abortion Is Not the Only Issue," *Christianity Today*, July 14, 1989.

Aryeh Spero
"Therefore Choose Life: How the Great Faiths View Abortion," *Policy Review*, Spring 1989.

John M. Swomley
"The Freedom to Choose," *Christian Social Action*, March 1991.

Can Abortion
Be Justified?

Chapter Preface

Approximately 1.6 million abortions are performed annually in the United States. The vast majority of these abortions are performed because women are too young or too poor to raise a child. Other women decide on abortion because they are without a partner, or they are in school or in a demanding career. Opinion polls indicate that the American public is ambivalent about abortion in these cases. Many people believe these reasons are too selfish or trivial to justify ending the life of an unborn child.

Americans are much less ambivalent about abortions in cases of rape, incest, serious fetal deformity, or when the life of the mother is threatened. The public tends to believe these circumstances can justify abortion. Kristin Luker, the author of *Abortion and the Politics of Motherhood*, writes that Americans "simultaneously approve of 'necessary' abortions and disapprove of 'casual' abortions."

The ambivalence many Americans feel about abortions complicates an already complex, emotional issue. The following chapter presents personal testimonies and arguments concerning when, if ever, abortion is justified.

"The act of cancelling an unplanned and unwanted pregnancy is a way of saying to that soul that their time has not yet arrived."

An Unwanted Child Justifies Abortion

K.B. Welton

Many people argue that it is wrong to deny abortions to women with unwanted pregnancies. Having an unwanted child, these people believe, can have a very detrimental impact on a woman's life. They also argue that unwanted children are more likely to suffer from parental abuse and other problems than wanted children. In the following viewpoint, K.B. Welton agrees with this argument. In addition, the author contends that the earth is so overcrowded that it is a greater sin not to abort unwanted children than it is to allow them to enter a world in which they will likely be disadvantaged and abused. Welton is the author of the book *Abortion Is Not a Sin*, from which this viewpoint is taken.

As you read, consider the following questions:

1. What does Welton mean by the statement "we are not slaves to the unborn"?
2. Why is the author critical of the role of the Catholic church in matters of abortion and contraception?
3. Why does Welton emphasize the importance of maternal instincts?

Excerpted from *Abortion Is Not a Sin* by K.B. Welton. Costa Mesa, CA: Pandit Press, Inc., 1987. Copyright 1987 by K.B. Welton.

These are new times. And we are no longer living in a world of only several hundred million people. It will soon be six billion people and more. It took mankind millions of years to reach the level of one billion people. And now that science has largely removed Mother Nature's hand from the scene, the earth's population has exploded, and in the last century alone, at an unprecedented rate. Mankind's miracles of disease control and food production, while solving some problems, have created others. To date, our technology has proved itself to be a two-edged sword.

In a brief moment of historical time, we have now filled the earth with our human species beyond our present political, economic, and perhaps environmental, capacity to properly care for all these individuals. Abortion in this setting is no longer a crime, it is a necessity. Freedom to choose *not* to give birth is essential, and no choice but to give birth may be called immoral. . . .

The Sexual Revolution

Since the advent of the pill and other modern methods of contraception, we now have options in our sexual lives that mankind never had before. Sex has come out of the closet. The genie is out of the bottle. With birth control, we have divorced the reproductive process from pure amative love and our raucous genital copulation. In other words, we can enjoy one another now, provided we act like responsible human beings occupying a fragile and overcrowded planet. But those who do not act responsibly, or for other reasons find themselves unwillingly pregnant, must not then be forced to aggravate our population problems in the name of short-term mercy and compassion that only adds to our larger problems.

> But if God had wanted us to think with our wombs, why did
> he give us a brain?
>
> Clare Boothe Luce

Even with the current wave of sexually transmitted diseases, which has often been another one of Mother Nature's ways to control population, we will sooner or later discover the cure for these problems. And even severely altered social mores, as a result of sexually transmitted diseases, will not eliminate excessive population growth and the real need for terminating unwanted pregnancies. The sexual revolution unleashed by the birth control pill, and newer devices on the horizon, is here to stay. But "accidents" will always happen.

As men and women, we were made to love one another. God even gave us children to show us we were doing it right. The problem is that we just don't need so many proofs! The sexual revolution and modern technology enable us to fulfill our human needs in intimacy and sexual contact. They have also given us the ability to plan our future and prepare for one of life's great gifts—a loved and wanted child.

Today, in these new and different times, each birth must be given the utmost care and forethought. We must do unto others as we would have them do unto us in bringing our children into this world. If we care so little about the birth of a child that we let it happen by accident, and at a time when we are not prepared, or mature enough for the daily and almost life-long demands of parenthood, then we need to deeply consider the process of delaying a soul's incarnation into our lives.

Abortion Is Moral in Unwanted Pregnancies

[I] feel abhorrence for the idea of deliberately bringing an unwanted pregnancy to term, delivering forth a helpless human being, and then just giving it away to others to care for. To never again take any responsibility whatsoever for a baby deliberately brought into this world seems to me utterly barbaric!

By contrast, abortion is absolutely moral and responsible. To stop the pregnancy and prevent the birth of a child who cannot be properly cared for shows wisdom—and understanding of the realities of life. The only life in an embryo is the woman's life within it. Until it can live a separate life, it is *not* a separate life. "Infallible" doctrines and dogmas simply wither away in the light of that fact.

Constance Robertson, *The Religious Case for Abortion*, 1983.

And this is not just for selfish motives, but for the best interests of the unborn and our world. Our being considerate of current conditions and attentive to the long-term interests of the unborn cannot now be said to be selfish. On the contrary, it is compassionate. As one young woman, on a radio talk show, expressed her feelings about her abortion years before at an immature age: "I feel good that I am not being a bad parent."

We Are Not Slaves to the Unborn

And even in the absence of the important social and environmental considerations, who is to say that we don't have a right to plan the entrance of the new soul into our bodies, which he or she will use for their own reincarnation. We are not slaves to the unborn, we are their mothers and fathers. We might say they borrow our genetic material and use the womb for their own purposes—it is the new soul's staging ground. But can we not also say that it is both our duty, and an act of compassion, to set the stage and prepare, in our own time, for the right occasion to give birth?

The act of cancelling an unplanned and unwanted pregnancy is a way of saying to that soul that their time has not yet arrived. It is a prayerful and respectful assuming of responsibility for unplanned and untimely pregnancies, and we might well say for the good of the soul's eventual life to be. There is nothing wrong in taking control of one's reproductive life. And yet women are still punished by the Church, and many countries of the world, first for exercising their own sexuality, and secondly for taking responsibility for unwanted procreation. Why?

> The first right of every child is to be wanted, to be desired, to be planned with an intensity of love that gives it its title to being.

> Margaret Sanger

Only when the mother isn't forced into motherhood can she truly love and nourish her child. If we assume a fetal "right-to-life" we also assume the new soul is willing to make a slave of the mother against her will. And any outside interference or coercion in this intuitive connection can only sour a delicate relationship between mother and child. After impregnation by a male who did not intend to become a father, and when a woman seeks help with her problem pregnancy, the reluctant mother often encounters the phalanx of moralist male ideologues . . . hypocrites without wombs seeking to enforce motherhood. Going "underground" for help is a necessity in some countries even today. . . .

The Role of the Catholic Church

Unfortunately, the role of the Church has been to prevent and frighten young women from using contraception, almost insuring that they will have unwanted babies in their early sexual experiments. And just as the Church, in effect, [causes] unwanted pregnancies and therefore abortions, it then condemns the young mothers and tells them they will now be excommunicated and go to hell if they have an abortion. Is this trap moral? Also, in too many cases, the Church does little or nothing to provide for these unfortunate children that their policies have helped to create!

Millions of families, and the many children that result from unregulated procreation, are becoming dependent on public assistance in cities around the world. Millions now grow up in poverty and miss an equal chance in life. And the sad fact is they are likely to repeat the mistakes of their parents at an even earlier age, thus intensifying the pace of irresponsible demands upon their community and the world.

Often it appears that in all too many cases the only mission of the Church seems to be to baptize the children and train them to be good Catholics, who will then go on to repeat the same sad experience of not using birth control, getting pregnant at an age when they are unable to properly provide for the child, and thus creating another disadvantaged being on the earth who will most likely require public and private assistance in his or her life. Whatever the intent, this is the unfortunate effect of policies.

Women Need to Live Reasonable Lives

Here are some reasons why friends of mine had abortions: they were in college and wanted to graduate. They were in graduate school or professional training and wanted to finish. They could not care for a child and keep their jobs. They were not in a relationship that could sustain parenthood at that time. They were not, in short, ready or able to be good mothers yet, although those who have children are good mothers now. Hard-hearted calculations of "convenience"? Only if you think that pregnancy is the price of sex, that women have no work but motherhood, and that children don't need grown-up parents.

The fact is, when your back is to the wall of unwanted pregnancy, it doesn't matter whether or not you think the fetus is a person. That's why, in this country, Roman Catholic women, who are less likely to use effective birth control, have a higher abortion rate than Jews or Protestants. Women do what they need to do in order to lead reasonable lives, and they always have.

Katha Pollitt, *The New York Times Magazine*, November 20, 1988.

The cycle goes on year after year and Mother Earth, in many countries, is now breaking under the assault of new life. This is unconscious, unplanned and largely unwanted humanity, that in the spiritual scheme of things will most likely not provide us with the strong, healthy, and properly cared for future stewards of spaceship earth. This truly vicious cycle must stop if we are to see any progress in our world. Only contraception, abortion and family planning are the realistic weapons in our continuing battle for population balance.

Mandatory Motherhood

The Catholic church, and all other fundamentalist religions around the world that still oppose and prevent the use of contraception and abortion, in effect, favor "mandatory motherhood." For whatever reason or mistake the conception has occurred, where abortion is outlawed, a woman is effectively condemned to give birth against her will. It wasn't long ago that women were burned at the stake for attempting to define their own feminist cosmology. It seems that in past ages, as is somewhat true today, a "witch" was any who had the guts to tell the Church to stay out of her life.

Today, the Church cannot burn women at the stake, but its doctrines are mental torture enough on those who choose to disagree but lack the necessary philosophical strength and independence to combat the guilt and condemnation. The real problem is that young women are, in effect, punished into giving birth for having engaged in sex. Thus does the child become the punishment. This is not compassion for the unborn but control of the living, a distinct lack of compassion for the woman's right to choose and control her reproduction. And this policy is why so many women today are leaving the Church.

> How can we justify compulsory pregnancy? Here we are strapping down a living and breathing creature (the mother) and then forcing her to give birth in the unproven belief that we are saving a "life." In many cases we are ruining two lives, the mother's and the baby.
>
> Garrett Hardin

Is not this one-sided definition of compassion, that commands the birth of unplanned and unwanted children, not ruining the lives of the mother and the child as well? What really happens to these mostly unwanted and unplanned babies, after the birth event, when the moralists have faded away to spread their compassion elsewhere? As might be expected, many studies from around the world now indicate that all is not well with unplanned and unwanted children. There are far too many teenage "parents" now coerced into aborting their own futures, and their children's, by giving birth when they themselves are still dependent and unable to provide a decent home for the newborn.

> In a Swedish study 120 children born after refusal by the authorities to grant permission for abortion were compared to paired controls of the same sex born either in the same hospital or district to mothers who had not applied for abortion.
>
> After a close observation for 21 years, the former group of children were found to have higher incidences of psychiatric disorder, delinquency, criminal behavior, and alcoholism. They were more often recipients of public welfare, were more unfit for military service, and received less schooling than those of the controls.
>
> In another study of 213 children born to women who had been refused therapeutic abortion, the unwanted children were shown to be physically as well as mentally impaired.
>
> Hans and Thuwe Forssman
> *The Abortion Experience*

It is not hard to understand why these studies appear to confirm the real disadvantages of children born from unwanted pregnancies. They also tell us something about the instincts of mothers. Might we not say that most mothers intuitively sense when the time is not right, or even that the baby may not be well, and thus decide to terminate an unwanted and unplanned pregnancy? And subconsciously, in her intuitive maternal wisdom, a pregnant woman may sense that something is wrong with the pregnancy, for whatever reason. However, if society attempts to crush a woman's instincts, and prevent the best of all possible births, we do a great disservice to the woman, her children, and all of humanity.

And what can we say of the mentality, and morality, that demands that a woman have a baby simply because she has become pregnant? Is not the how and the why of the pregnancy of any importance? The panicked and unprepared "mother" is now doomed to motherhood against her will—and her child is her punishment. In the case of teenage pregnancy this is especially reprehensible and counterproductive. And what are we doing for, or to, this new child in the most negative of circumstances? Are we saving his or her life? Are we saving the mother's life? Or ruining them both? . . .

With unwanted pregnancies, abortion saves the life of the mother, giving her the chance to position her children in her life so as to maximize the conditions for the welfare of the child, the mother, her village and our world.

"There is no such thing as an unwanted child—there are only unwanting people among those who are born."

An Unwanted Child Does Not Justify Abortion

Stephen Schwarz

Stephen Schwarz is professor of philosophy at the University of Rhode Island in Kingston and an opponent of abortion. In the following viewpoint, Schwarz argues that the unborn child's right to life should take precedence over whether or not it is wanted. Schwarz further contends that many supposedly unwanted children are eventually accepted by their natural or adoptive parents and go on to lead happy and contented lives. He also believes that even if an unwanted child grows up unhappy, it should be his or her decision to end that unhappy life.

As you read, consider the following questions:

1. Do you agree with Schwarz that there is no such thing as an unwanted child? Why or why not?
2. What does the author mean by the statement "the obligation to not kill a person clearly overrides the obligation to benefit a person"?
3. How does the author justify his belief that abortion and child abuse go together?

Excerpted from *The Moral Question of Abortion,* by Stephen Schwarz. Used by permission of Loyola University Press, Chicago, Illinois.

Abortion is usually thought of as a procedure to benefit the woman. But it is also advocated in the name of benefiting the child. . . .

[Joseph Fletcher has] argued: "Every child should be a wanted child. We should not bring an unwanted child into the world. It is not fair to him; he is better off if he is not born. He will have a miserable life, rejected by his parents, unloved. For his own sake, he should be spared such a life. Abortion, in such cases, is the merciful termination of a pregnancy that, if continued, will result in an unloved, miserably unhappy child. Abortion is the only humane thing to do in such a case."

We must certainly have the greatest sympathy for a child who is unloved and rejected. We should do all in our power to alleviate her suffering. We should love her in a special way, and try, as far as possible, to make up for the love she has not received. These are the things we should do—not kill her by an abortion.

"We should not bring an unwanted child into the world," [states Fletcher.] But the child in the womb is already in the world! The womb is part of the world. It is a part of the woman's body, and she is surely in the world. What is in the womb is just as much already in the world as the womb itself. Thus, the child in the womb is as much here as her mother. She is merely not visible to us, and we cannot interact with her. And so we overlook her. But she is as real, and as present, as the rest of us.

One cannot kill innocent person B for the sake of benefiting person A. The same is true when B is the supposed beneficiary. We cannot kill B for the sake of B. The obligation to not kill a person clearly overrides the obligation to benefit a person.

The Unwanted Child Can Become Wanted

A child unwanted in his preborn phase may become wanted later. How many times have we heard of women with unplanned pregnancies, on the one hand considering abortions, on the other hand rejecting the idea of keeping the baby now and then giving him up for adoption after birth? The same child, unwanted as a baby in the womb, will then be very much wanted when he has emerged from the womb, when he can be seen and touched, when it is psychologically easier to identify with him. This is especially true when it is the pregnancy that is unwanted, and when the child is called "unwanted" because of this. [According to Thomas Hilgers and colleagues,] there is evidence to suggest that "most women who are refused abortion will be glad that they carried the pregnancy to term."

A child unwanted by his natural mother even after his birth may be wanted by others eager to adopt him. Thousands of couples would like to adopt babies. So few are available, and usually only after a very long waiting period. How tragic that at the same time a million and a half or more are slaughtered each year by abortion! . . .

Suppose, despite this, that the child remains unwanted and unhappy. Even then the argument for abortion does not hold. For it says we should kill preborn children who will be unwanted or unhappy. Should we then not also kill other children who are unwanted? If, as the pro-abortion reasoning assumes, killing the preborn child who will be unwanted is doing him a favor by sparing him a life of misery, why not grant this favor also to other children? If preborn persons should be killed to save them from a life of misery, the same logic should apply also to postborn persons.

Don Meredith. Reprinted with permission.

If there seems to be a difference between killing an unwanted born person and abortion, it is, I think, largely because of the assumption that we should not bring an unwanted child into the world. To regain our perspective we have only to remember that the child in the womb is already in the world!

Perhaps an unwanted child would not want to continue living. Perhaps he would decide that life in his particular condition is not worth living. It is one thing if he decides this for himself; it is quite another if we decide this for him, if we impose this awesome life and death decision on him. How dare we force such a decision on the child, the irreversible decision that a life in an unhappy state is a life not worth living!

The person recommending abortion in such cases should ask himself how he would feel if someone else forced such a decision on him. He would want his autonomy respected. He would claim the right to make such a decision himself. The child's autonomy should also be respected, as well as his right to decide. Why is he not allowed to live until he is capable of making his own decision?

Many persons who suffered through an unhappy childhood find happiness, meaning, and fulfillment later in life, through creativity, love, and many other things. The present argument for abortion assumes that an unwanted child will be an unhappy person. This is an unwarranted assumption, and when it is removed, the pro-abortion argument collapses.

The term *unwanted* seems to be an adjective modifying *child*. It is not. The child does not change her characteristics if she is first unwanted then wanted, or the reverse. We change. We should change from unwanting to wanting people.

So the whole problem of the unwanted child is our problem. There is nothing wrong with an unwanted child, no reason why she should be destroyed. There is very much of a problem with unwanting parents and an unwanting society. The changes that are called for to solve this problem are changes in us, not changes in the so-called unwanted child, from being alive to being destroyed.

There is no such thing as an unwanted child—there are only unwanting people among those who are born.

Abortion and Child Abuse

It is argued: "Abortion is necessary to prevent, or at least to minimize, the terrible evil of child abuse. Anyone who has ever witnessed the absolute horror of child abuse cannot but wish that such a child had never been born."

As in the previous type of case, we must have the greatest sympathy for a child who is a victim of child abuse. We must do all we can to stop this abomination. But to kill the child before he is born?

First, abortion is not a solution for child abuse, because abortion is itself the ultimate child abuse! Recall . . . the horror of the methods of abortion, such as saline burning of the skin for one to two hours or cutting the child to pieces, and the pain these methods cause to the child. Even by other "clean and painless" methods, abortion would still be child abuse because all murder is a form of abuse.

Second, abortion is not a solution for child abuse. It is simply false to assume that it is the unwanted child who will be abused while the wanted child will not. That is, abortion for this purpose, even if it were justified, would not be effective. "Many studies have demonstrated that the victim of child abuse is *not* the 'unwanted child.'" It is the wanted child. In his study of child abuse, Edward F. Lenoski, M.D., found that "91% of the parents admitted they wanted the child they had abused. The mothers had also donned maternity clothing two months earlier than most expectant mothers." Furthermore [according to Lenoski]: "A higher percentage of the abused children were named after one of the parents," indicating that they were wanted.

No Such Thing as an Unwanted Child

Abortion advocates insist that abortion "saves unwanted children" from living miserable lives. But most unplanned pregnancies actually end up very much wanted. In fact, no child is ever truly "unwanted," as is proven by the great surplus of loving people who desperately want to adopt children. "Unwantedness" is simply not a trait of children. Instead, if there is a problem, it lies with "unwanting" adults.

David C. Reardon, *Aborted Women: Silent No More*, 1987.

Third, there is another compelling reason why abortion is not a solution for child abuse. [As David C. Reardon points out,] "instead of reducing the incidence of child abuse, the evidence shows that abortion actually *increases* child abuse." There are a number of reasons for this:

1. The abused child is reduced to an object. [According to Reardon:]

> The abortion mentality reinforces the attitude of treating children like objects, objects that can be wanted or unwanted according to whether or not "it" satisfies parental needs. . . . What aborters and abusers have in common . . . is "the assumption that the rights, desires, and ideas of the adult take full precedence over those of the child, and that children are essentially the property of parents who have the right to deal with their offspring as they see fit, without interference."

2. The abused child is a victim of the result of guilt. [Reardon comments that] "aborted women frequently feel guilt, and 'guilt is one of the major factors causing battering and infanticide.' This guilt results in 'intolerable feelings of self-hatred, which the parent takes out on the child.'"

3. The abused child is a victim of the result of lowered self-esteem. [Again, according to Reardon,] "child abusers almost invariably have a significant lack of self-esteem. Since lowered self-esteem is a well-documented aftermath of abortion, the ex-

perience of abortion may help shape an emotional environment which is conducive to the battering of other or later children."

Lenoski states that if the mother sees a resemblance of herself in her child, and if "the mother has very little self-esteem, she will see in the baby a reflection of the low self-esteem she feels toward herself," making the child a potential victim of the bad feelings the mother has for herself.

4. The abused child is a victim of the result of failures in bonding. Dr. Philip G. Ney, an authority on child abuse, explains:

> It would appear that those who abort their infants at any stage of pregnancy interrupt a very delicate mechanism and sever the developing bond that is critical for the infant's protection against the mother's carelessness or rage. It is hypothesized that, once bonding is interrupted in the primipara, there are long-lasting psychological changes which make it more difficult for the same bond to develop in subsequent pregnancies. For this reason, it is likely that abortion contributes to bonding failure, an important cause of child battering. Consequently, as rates of abortion increase, rates of battering will increase proportionately.

5. The abused child is a victim of the results of marital stress. [As Reardon states:]

> The marital stress caused by abortion increases family hostilities and thus heightens the possibility of violent outbreaks. If the father felt left out of the abortion decision or only resentfully agreed to the abortion, or if the woman felt pressured into the abortion by her mate, deep feelings of resentment and violation of trust might cause frequent eruption of emotions. In the heat of such parental disputes, children are likely to get caught in the crossfire, objects of release for the pent-up rage of adults.

6. The abused child is a victim of the results of abortion, because, as Dr. Ney states:

> 1. Abortion decreases an individual's instinctual restraint against the occasional rage felt toward those dependent on his or her care.
> 2. Permissive abortion diminishes the social taboo against aggressing [against] the defenseless.
> 3. Abortion increases the hostility between generations.
> 4. Abortion has devalued children, thus diminishing the value of caring for children. . . .

Abortion and child abuse go together. Each represents the loss of reverence for a human person, the willingness to use violence against him. Even when abortion and child abuse are not practiced by the same persons, they are manifestations of the same underlying attitude of loss of respect for human persons, and thus they tend to exist together. Again, abortion is not a solution to the terrible problem of child abuse; it is part of that problem.

"For us, the diagnosis of Down syndrome was reason to choose abortion."

Congenital Disorders Justify Abortion

Rayna Rapp

Even when a pregnancy is a welcomed, planned event, the issue of abortion can still loom large. With many women postponing childbirth until their thirties and even forties, the probability of birth defects and congenital disease rises. Because of this, many women undergo sophisticated prenatal testing to determine whether the fetus suffers from any abnormalities. If the test results are positive and the woman is carrying an abnormal fetus, she may elect to have an abortion. In the following viewpoint, Rayna Rapp explains how she discovered her unborn child had Down syndrome, a congenital disorder characterized by mental retardation. Rapp chose to abort rather than carry the pregnancy to term. Rapp is chair of the anthropology department at the New School for Social Research in New York City.

As you read, consider the following questions:

1. While the author explains that she admires women who choose to have a baby even though it is handicapped, she chose not to. Why not?
2. How was the author's experience different from her husband's?
3. If you were faced with this decision, what would you do? Why?

Excerpted from Rayna Rapp, "Dimensions of Legal Abortion" in Rita Arditti (ed.), *Test Tube Women: What Future for Motherhood?* (Boston: Unwin Hyman, 1984) © 1984 by Unwin Hyman. Reprinted by permission.

Mike called the fetus XYLO, XY for its unknown sex, LO for the love we were pouring into it. Day by day we fantasized about who this growing cluster of cells might become. Day by day, we followed the growth process in the myriad books that surround modern pregnancy for the over-thirty-five baby boomlet. Both busy with engrossing work and political commitments, we welcomed this potential child with excitement, fantasy, and the rationality of scientific knowledge. As a Women's Movement activist, I had decided opinions about treating pregnancy as a normal, not a diseased condition, and we were fortunate to find a health-care team—obstetrician, midwives, genetic counselor—who shared that view.

The early months of the pregnancy passed in a blur of exhaustion and nausea. Preoccupied with my own feelings, I lived in a perpetual underwater, slow-motion version of my prior life. As one friend put it, I was already operating on fetal time, tied to an unfamiliar regimen of enforced naps, loss of energy, and rigid eating. Knowing the research on nutrition, on hormones, and on miscarriage rates among older pregnant women, I did whatever I could to stay comfortable.

I was thirty-six when XYLO was conceived, and like many of my peers, I chose to have amniocentesis, a prenatal test for birth defects such as Down syndrome, Tay-Sachs disease, and sickle-cell anemia. Both Mike and I knew about prenatal diagnosis from our friends' experiences, and from reading about it. Each year, many thousands of American women choose amniocentesis to detect birth defects. The procedure is performed between the sixteenth and twentieth weeks of pregnancy. Most obstetricians, mine included, send their pregnant patients directly to the genetic division of a hospital where counseling is provided, and the laboratory technicians are specially trained. Analysis of amniotic fluid requires complex laboratory work, and can cost between five hundred dollars and two thousand dollars.

Fear of Down Syndrome

It was fear of Down syndrome that sent us to seek prenatal diagnosis of XYLO. Down syndrome produces a characteristic physical appearance—short, stocky size, large tongue, puffy upward-slanting eyes with skin folds in the inner corners—and is a major cause of mental retardation, worldwide. People with Down syndrome are quite likely to have weak cardiovascular systems, respiratory problems, and run a greater risk of developing childhood leukemia. While the majority of Down syndrome infants used to die very young, a combination of antibiotics and infant surgery enables modern medicine to keep them alive. And programs of childhood physical-mental stimulation

138

may facilitate their assimilation. Some parents also opt for cosmetic surgery—an expensive and potentially risky procedure. Down syndrome is caused by an extra chromosome, at the twenty-first pair of chromosomes, as geneticists label them. And while the diagnosis of Down spells mental retardation and physical vulnerability, no geneticist can tell you how seriously affected your particular fetus will be. There is no cure for Down syndrome. A pregnant woman whose fetus is diagnosed as having the extra chromosome can either prepare to raise a mentally retarded and physically vulnerable child, or decide to abort it. . . .

Confronting the Decision to Abort

How could I bring this person, whose life expectancy was 60 years, into the world, watching him suffer and not understand? But how could I abort and live with my guilt? . . .

Unless the child was institutionalized, I would have to give up my teaching to be a full-time nurse, putting the entire financial burden on [my husband] Bud. We would have to begin saving immediately for that day, in our old age, when we could no longer care for the child at home. While we might have somehow coped had we never had the tests, Bud couldn't fathom knowingly bringing these burdens upon us. . . . I decided I must go through with the abortion to preserve my family.

Maria Vida Hunt, *McCall's*, July 1985.

The waiting period for amniocentesis results is a long one, and I was very anxious. Cells must be cultured, then analyzed, a process that takes two to four weeks. We wait, caught between the late date at which amniocentesis can be performed (usually sixteen to twenty weeks); the moment of quickening, when the woman feels the fetus move (roughly eighteen to twenty weeks); and the legal limits of abortion (very few of which are performed after twenty-four weeks in the United States). Those of my friends who have had amniocentesis report terrible fantasies, dreams, and crying fits, and I was no exception: I dreamed in lurid detail of my return to the lab, of awful damage. I woke up frantic, sobbing, to face the nagging fear that is focused in the waiting period after amniocentesis.

For the 98 percent of women whose amniotic fluid reveals no anomaly, reassurance arrives by phone, or more likely, by mail, confirming a negative test. When Nancy [the author's genetic counselor] called me twelve days after the tap, I began to scream as soon as I recognized her voice; in her office, I knew only positive results (very negative results, from a potential parent's point of view) are reported by phone. The image of myself, alone, screaming into a white plastic telephone is indelible. Although it only took twenty minutes to locate Mike and bring him and a close friend to my side, time is suspended in my memory. I replay the call, and my screams echo for indefinite periods. We learned, after contacting our midwives and obstetrician, that a diagnosis of a male fetus with Down syndrome had been made. Our fantasies for XYLO, our five months' fetus, were completely shattered.

Mike and I had discussed what we would do if amniocentesis revealed a serious genetic condition long before the test. For us, the diagnosis of Down syndrome was reason to choose abortion. Our thinking was clear, if abstract, long before the question became reality. We were eager to have a child, and prepared to change our lives to make emotional, social, and economic resources available. But the realities of raising a child who could never grow to independence would call forth more than we could muster, unless one or both of us gave up our work, our political commitments, our social existence beyond the household. And despite a shared commitment to coparenting, we both understood that in this society, that one was likely to be the mother. When I thought about myself, I knew that in such a situation, I would transform myself to become the kind of twenty-four-hour-a-day advocate such a child would require. I'd do the best and most loving job I could, and I'd undoubtedly become an activist in support of the needs of disabled children.

No Support for the Disabled

But other stark realities confronted us: to keep a Down syndrome child alive through potentially lethal health problems is an act of love with weighty consequences. As we ourselves age, to whom would we leave the person XYLO would become? Neither Mike nor I have any living kin who are likely to be young enough, or close enough, to take on this burden after our deaths. In a society where the state provides virtually no decent, humane services for the mentally retarded, how could we take responsibility for the future of our dependent Down syndrome child? In good conscience, we couldn't choose to raise a child who would become a ward of the state. The health care, schools, various therapies that Down syndrome children require are inadequately available, and horrendously expensive in America; no single family should have to shoulder all the burdens that a decent health and social policy may someday extend to physically and mentally disabled people. In the meantime, while struggling for such a society, we did not choose to bring a child into this world who could never grow up to care for himself.

Most women who've opted for amniocentesis are prepared to face the question of abortion, and many of us *do* choose it, after a diagnosis of serious disability is made. Perhaps 95 percent of Down syndrome pregnancies are terminated after test results are known. Reports on other diseases and conditions are harder to find, but in one study, the diagnosis of spina bifida led to abortion about 90 percent of the time.

A Nightmare Begins

A person's life can be turned into a nightmare with just a few words. My obstetrician was on the line, informing me that the results of the amniocentesis indicated the baby was severely abnormal, with forty-seven chromosomes instead of the normal forty-six. . . .

I managed to live through the day until [my husband] Jim came home. After much discussion and soul-searching, we decided that termination of the pregnancy was the only course. Every person deserves a fair chance at a good life, and this child wouldn't have that chance. He would also be an outcast, the object of stares and pity, perhaps even ridicule. He would never be a playmate for Jennifer [our daughter]; instead he'd be a lifelong burden, a burden we had no right to place on her. We had a responsibility to provide Jennifer with as normal and happy a childhood as possible, and we would be failing in that responsibility if we brought this child into the world. We knew that we couldn't cope with the havoc and devastation that visits families with children who are severely deformed and retarded.

Julie K. Ivey, *Glamour,* May 1982.

In shock and grief, I learned from my obstetrician that two kinds of late second-trimester abortions were available. Most common are the "installation procedures"—saline solution or urea is injected into the uterus to kill the fetus, and drugs are sometimes used to bring on labor. The woman then goes through labor to deliver the fetus. The second kind of mid-trimester abortion, and the one I chose, is a D&E—dilation and evacuation. This procedure demands more active intervention from a doctor, who vacuums out the amniotic fluid, and then removes the fetus. The D&E requires some intense, upsetting work for the medical team, but it's over in about twenty minutes, without putting the woman through labor. Both forms of late abortion entail some physical risk, and the psychological pain is enormous. Deciding to end the life of a fetus you've wanted and carried for most of five months is no easy matter. The number of relatively late second-trimester abortions performed for genetic reasons is very small. It seems an almost inconsequential number, unless you happen to be one of them.

Making the medical arrangements, going back for counseling, the pretests, and finally, the abortion, was the most difficult period of my adult life. I was then twenty-one weeks pregnant, and had been proudly carrying my expanding belly. Telling everyone—friends, family, students, colleagues, neighbors—seemed an endless nightmare. But it also allowed us to rely on their love and support during this terrible time. Friends streamed in from all over to teach my classes; I have scores of letters expressing concern; the phone never stopped ringing for weeks. Our community was invaluable, reminding us that our lives were rich and filled with love despite this loss. A few weeks afterward, I spoke with another woman who'd gone through selective abortion (as this experience is antiseptically called in medical jargon). She'd returned to work immediately, her terrible abortion experience unspoken. Colleagues assumed she'd had a late miscarriage, and didn't speak about it. Her isolation only underlined my appreciation of the support I'd received.

A Need for Support Services

My parents flew a thousand miles to sit guard over my hospital bed, answer telephones, shop, and cook. Filled with sorrow for the loss of their first grandchild, my mother told me of a conversation she'd had with my father. Despite their grief, they were deeply grateful for the test. After all, she reasoned, we were too young and active to be devastated like this; if the child had been born, she and my dad would have taken him to raise in their older years, so we could get on with raising other children. I can only respond with deep love and gratitude for the wellspring of compassion behind that conversation. But surely, no single woman, mother or grandmother, no single family, nuclear or extended, should have to bear all the burdens that raising a seriously disabled child entails. It points out, once again, the importance of providing decent, humane attention and services for other-than-fully-abled children and adults.

And, of course, parents of disabled children are quick to point out that the lives they've nurtured have been worth living. I honor their hard work and commitments, as well as their love, and I think that part of "informed consent" to amniocentesis and selective abortion should include information about parents' groups of Down syndrome children, and social services available to them, not just the individual, medical diagnosis of the problem. And even people who feel they could never choose a late abortion may nonetheless want amniocentesis so they'll have a few extra months to prepare themselves, other family members, friends, and special resources for the birth of a child with special, complex needs.

Recovering from the abortion took a long time. Friends, family, coworkers, students did everything they could to ease me through the experience. Even so, I yearned to talk with someone who'd "been there." Over the next few months, I used my personal and medical networks to locate and talk with a handful of other women who'd opted for selective abortions. In each case, I was the first person they'd ever met with a similar experience. The isolation of this decision and its consequences is intense. Only when women (and concerned men) speak of the experience of selective abortion as a tragic but chosen fetal death can we as a community offer the support, sort out the ethics, and give the compassionate attention that such a loss entails.

For two weeks, Mike and I breathed as one person. His distress, loss, and concern were never one whit less than my own. But we were sometimes upset and angered by the unconscious attitudes toward his loss. He was expected to "cope," while I was nurtured through my "need." We've struggled for male responsibility in birth control, sexual mutuality, childbirth, and child-rearing, and I think we need to acknowledge that those men who do engage in such transformed practices have mourning rights during a pregnancy loss, as well.

Different Experiences

Nonetheless, our experiences *were* different, and I'm compelled to recognize the material reality of my experience. Because it happened in my body, a woman's body, I recovered much more slowly than Mike did. By whatever mysterious process, he was able to damp back the pain, and throw himself back into work after several weeks. For me, it took months. As long as I had the fourteen pounds of pregnancy weight to lose, as long as my aching breasts, filled with milk, couldn't squeeze into bras, as long as my tummy muscles protruded, I was confronted with the physical reality of being post-pregnant, without a child. Mike's support seemed inadequate; I was still in deep mourning while he seemed distant and cured. Only much later, when I began doing research on amniocentesis, did I find one study of the stresses and strains of selective abortion. In a small sample of couples, a high percentage separated or divorced following this experience. Of course, the same holds true after couples face a child's disablement, or child death. Still, I had no idea that deep mourning for a fetus could be so disorienting. Abortion after prenatal diagnosis has been kept a medical and private experience, so there is no common fund of knowledge or support to alert us as individuals, as couples, as families, as friends, to the aftermath our "freedom of choice" entails.

Which is why I've pierced my private pain to raise this issue.

As feminists, we need to speak from our seemingly private experience toward a social and political agenda. I'm suggesting we lift the veil of privacy and professionalism to explore issues of health care, abortion, and the right to choose death, as well as life, for our genetically disabled fetuses. If XYLO's story, a true story, has helped to make this a compelling issue for more than one couple, then his five short months of fetal life will have been a great gift.

"The idea that a mother might ever choose to have or not have her child based on knowing something about that child . . . defies all logic of the heart."

Congenital Disorders Do Not Justify Abortion

Christine Allison

Christine Allison is the author of *I'll Tell You a Story, I'll Sing You a Song,* and the mother of a child with Down syndrome, a congenital disorder characterized by mental retardation. In the following viewpoint, Allison explains that she refused prenatal tests to determine the presence of fetal abnormalities in her unborn child because she believes that a mother should accept her child unconditionally. Allison is horrified by the fact that the majority of Down babies are aborted before birth. She fears that these children will eventually be eliminated altogether because of recent medical advances in prenatal testing.

As you read, consider the following questions:

1. Do you agree with the author's decision to refuse all prenatal testing? Why or why not?
2. In what ways have the lives of Down children changed in the last two decades, according to the author?
3. Do you agree with the author that a mother should accept her child unconditionally? Why or why not?

Christine Allison, "A Child to Lead Us," *The Human Life Review,* Summer 1989. Reprinted with permission.

We have learned a lot since that afternoon when our daughter Chrissie, just a few minutes old, took our family by the hand and gently led us into the world of the handicapped. Chrissie was born with Down syndrome. A mysterious bit of chromosomal protein created her almond-shaped eyes, squared-off ears, tiny nose, and low muscle tone. It created some mental and physical retardation, but we don't yet know how much. It also caused a complex heart defect called Tetralogy of Fallot, which will require heart surgery. The odds are good, about twenty to one, that she will survive the surgery and will be restored to a practically normal existence.

Chrissie has it harder than most kids, and she will spend much of her life getting to a place that, for most people, is Square One. But because of great medical and scientific developments, she will get there. And though it will never be easy for her, none of the hurdles in Chrissie's future are even remotely more threatening than what she has already survived. Four out of five Down syndrome babies die in miscarriage during the first trimester. Those miraculous few who are not miscarried must then face the considerably-worse odds of surviving "prenatal testing." The world of prenatal testing is without doubt the most perilous of all: a place where a child may find an adversary even in his own mother.

A Terrible Irony

It is a terrible irony that the world which has given Chrissie the penultimate—a chance to live a normal life—is the same world that may well extinguish the last person of her kind. But these are the terms of the new medicine. Over the past two decades, while one branch of the medical sciences has sought with extraordinary success to eradicate the worst effects of retardation in Down syndrome people, another branch has sought simply to eradicate people with Down syndrome. The forces of the latter have introduced a new prenatal test, easily administered and predicted to cut the Down syndrome newborn population by 90 percent in the United States. The next time you see a Down syndrome person sweeping a McDonald's or bagging groceries or riding in a yellow school bus with "normal" children, look hard. You are looking at a dying species.

Prenatal testing, just a few years ago, seemed a peripheral matter, an option unevenly offered to women of educational or financial privilege. I had always thought those tests were for the kind of people who get prenuptial agreements, as if love—or life—ought to come with a receipt. This is no longer the case: prenatal testing is now the medical rule, rather than an idle option. Amniocentesis for pregnant women who are 35 or older is now recommended just as surely as milk-drinking is. But am-

146

niocentesis is an abortion sentence for any child discovered in utero to be "flawed." I recall how the conversation came to a screeching halt when I casually announced to my obstetrician that I was not going to take any of "the tests." It was a major breach of patient's etiquette, to be sure, and what followed was a form of intimidation that an unresolved mother might not have survived. Surely, a Down syndrome fetus would not have survived.

A Perfect Child: Not Constitutionally Guaranteed

Lots of women—and they keep increasing in number—have abortions for reasons that have nothing whatever to do with how much money they have. . . .

Especially now that more women under 35 are undergoing amniocentesis, the choice is abortion because the kid down there is going to be retarded. Or the kid has some other defect. And since everyone wants a perfect baby—it's guaranteed in the Constitution, isn't it?—the kid is done away with.

Nat Hentoff, *The Village Voice*, October 2, 1984.

Of course, while we were assuaging our respective consciences, neither my doctor nor I knew that deep within my womb an extra chromosome was informing each cell in Chrissie's body as to who she was and who she would be. As I have learned since her birth, Chrissie is not a normal person who was twisted by genetic mishap. Every cell in her body is different from every cell in yours and mine. This is not to say she is inhuman. She is, quite simply, another biological version of the human species. Certainly a slower version, and certainly a gentler one. In that sense, she is perfectly who she is.

But there is more to know about Chrissie and those like her. And mothers, especially those over 35, know little but their own fears on the subject. For the 35-plus mother, Down syndrome is different from the other genetic and neurological errors that might befall their newborn; most mothers understand very clearly that the chances of having a Down child relate directly to age and that the odds get significantly worse each year.

The chances of bearing a Down syndrome child at 35 are one in 370; at 38, one in 173; at 40, one in 106. The syndrome is not hereditary; that is, it does not "run" in families. It is a disorder that has escaped all scientific explanation, except for the fact that it occurs more frequently with older mothers and fathers.

However top-of-mind Down syndrome is for the pregnant 35-plus mother, most (through no fault of their own) have little understanding of what it means to have the syndrome today. It is this basic ignorance that makes the climate ripe for the quiet genocide that is taking place. Indeed, so much has changed in the past twenty years that books and tracts on the subject published before 1980 are considered utterly unreliable. (In 1970, the Encyclopedia Britannica included a Down syndrome child under the heading "monster.") Many people still believe such babies are routinely sent to institutions at birth. The truth is that one would be hard pressed to find an institution that would accept a Down syndrome baby today.

A Revolution in Treating Down Children

To understand the revolution that has taken place in the world of Down syndrome, one must go back to the late 1960s, when the fashionable "nature versus nurture" arguments were being waged in college classrooms and manifested in social programs like "Headstart." Parents and child-development specialists and therapists started working with "at-risk" children in "early intervention" programs. Early intervention for Down children consisted of targeted sensory bombardment: intense mental, physical and emotional stimulation designed to escort the children through normal development stages and to reduce unnecessary delays. Speech therapy began in the first week. Physical therapy from birth modified the impact of low muscle tone and lax ligaments. Occupational therapy and special education developed self-help and cognitive skills. It was a far cry from the desolate state-institution walls most lived their lives within, and the children responded. They began to read and write. And sometimes they were writing poetry.

Chrissie, at age 14 months, has already spent a year attending the New York League for Early Learning at Teachers College, Columbia University. At twelve months, she tested developmentally at ten months. She understands most of what is said to her, obeys commands and is just starting to use her sign language. Her prognosis for continued education in a "regular" school is excellent but neither she nor the kind of attention she is receiving is unusual.

All Down syndrome children, regardless of their parents' backgrounds or financial circumstances, receive from state-financed programs the benefits of early intervention. There is no such thing as not being able to "afford" a Down syndrome child: every bit of therapy and special education is paid for by the state. The education is there, it is available for all—and it works. Indeed, the first generation of Down syndrome people to have experienced this extraordinary brand of preparation are causing medical books to be rewritten, and then rewritten again.

Of course, none of this changes the fact that Down syndrome

is still the leading cause of mental retardation in this country, or the even more difficult fact that many serious physical complications often accompany it. What *has* changed is the medical community's ability to repair the distressed organs and stave off the kind of diseases that only a few years ago would have brought about an early demise for the Down syndrome person. Unquestionably, these children spend more time in the hospital than normal children. But these days, they are attaining an average life expectancy of 55 years. The hard part is Getting Born.

Prenatal Testing

Until recently, a pregnant woman over 35 had three basic tests to choose from: the alpha fetoprotein test, the chorionic villus sampling and amniocentesis. For all pregnant women, regardless of age, doctors already routinely obtain alpha fetoprotein samples in the 16th week to test for neural tube defects; this is done by screening blood samples from the mother and in no way does it endanger the fetus. The chorionic villus test involves the risk of miscarriage for the fetus. It is performed in the seven-to-ten-week period, and involves snipping fetal cells from the developing placenta for genetic analysis. Amniocentesis also presents the risk of miscarriage; it requires a needle sample of the amniotic fluid and is usually done at 16 to 18 weeks.

The risk of miscarriage has always put a damper on fetal testing—I remember the heartbreak of a neighbor who after years of "trying to get pregnant" had amniocentesis and lost her child—and this is why the chorionic villus sampling and amniocentesis are generally recommended only to women over 35, for whom the risk of miscarriage is, at that point, less than the risk of carrying a Down syndrome baby. The newer chorionic villus test was regarded as having the major advantage of time: early diagnosis of Down syndrome or other defects could result in an earlier abortion, with less physical and emotional "difficulty."

The result of all this has been life for Down syndrome babies: at present, 80 percent of all these babies are born to women *under* 35. But now, with the work of Dr. Nicholas J. Wald of the Medical College of St. Bartholomew's Hospital in London and his colleagues, including Dr. James B. Haddow in Scarborough, Maine, and Dr. Jacob A. Canick of Brown University in Rhode Island, the chances of a Down syndrome child making it to birth may be somewhere this side of impossible.

Dr. Wald and his associates have developed a prenatal testing procedure which examines the presence of three basic proteins in the pregnant mother's blood. Through an easy, "non-invasive" sampling, analysts can determine whether there is a strong likelihood of a Down syndrome baby because, in the 16th week, they produce abnormally large amounts of human chorionic go-nadotropin, and disproportionately smaller amounts of two fetal proteins (estriol and alpha fetoprotein). By measuring the protein levels in all pregnant women in the 16th week, doctors can determine whether the more conclusive amniocentesis test should be recommended. The risk of having an "unnecessary" amniocentesis is avoided and everyone—over and under 35—can be easily tested. The test, Dr. Wald anticipates, will soon be "pretty widespread."

Eugenic Abortions

The abortion of unborn children diagnosed as potentially handi-capped is frequently placed under the category of "therapeutic abortions." But selective abortions are not in any way therapeutic for the mothers and are certainly not therapeutic for the aborted children. The correct term for such abortions is *eugenic* abortions, where eugenic, in this case, means identifying and eliminating persons with "inferior" genes or those who are deemed capable of only an "inferior quality" of life.

David C. Reardon, *Aborted Women: Silent No More*, 1987.

Most women who choose to be tested will also choose to abort the baby if the test is positive. Some studies say the figure is 90 percent. There are now approximately 250,000 Down syndrome people living in the United States. Each year, four to five thousand Down babies are born. If the testing procedures and the consequential abortions become standard, that number would be reduced to 400 to 500 each year. To muddy matters even more, the women who test are more often than not the mothers of "wanted" babies. That is, I want you if you are the baby I want. The idea that a mother might ever choose to have or not have her child based on knowing something about that child —his I.Q., what he will look like, his emotional demeanor—de-fies all logic of the heart. But this is an age where even the risk of accepting one's own progeny, for better or worse, has become too much to contemplate. It is the end of romance if a mother will not unconditionally bear her own child. But it is something worse: an awful, mechanical fastidiousness fed by that school of medical science which forgets that its mandate is to heal. If pre-natal testing suggests that a human being might not be more than the sum of his imperfect parts, it tells *us* that only certain of us might qualify for life.

In one of the most poignant, fierce, and determined battles to live deeply and well, Down syndrome people are breaking through the walls of their own retardation and grasping their world. Yet as a species they appear to be doomed. Unlike those who would abort them, these Down people have accepted the dare of life, which is to live it. In California, an eleven-year-old Down syndrome girl writes her first line on a computer. She painstakingly taps out "I like God's finest whispers." In Brooklyn, a Down fifth-grader dashes off the bus to his mother with a report card from his yeshiva: he has earned average grades in all of his classes, and speaks and writes in three different languages.

And then there's our Chrissie, who last week crawled seven paces for the saltine cracker her dad held outstretched to her. She had been battling for that saltine for two months.

An unexpected gift, a gift out of season and for no reason, carries a special weight. When Chrissie was born, she was that unexpected gift. In the weeks that followed her arrival, we were bombarded with messages from friends and acquaintances about the majesty of a Down syndrome child; the words of our friends affirmed what was in our hearts. Chrissie is a blessing in a way a normal child is not. It is in describing her that the word "special" rises from banality and comes grippingly alive. That she may now be a member of the last generation of her kind, a group silently and methodically targeted for extinction, alarms my heart. Especially now, knowing as I do that when she is older, Chrissie will be able to read—and understand—what I have written.

"My wife and I took my daughter for the abortion and brought her home. The abortion was not a traumatic experience. It was an end to a traumatic experience."

Rape Justifies Abortion

Anonymous

In the following viewpoint, a well-known journalist recounts the story of his daughter's gang-rape, subsequent pregnancy, and abortion. The author, who prefers to remain anonymous to protect his daughter's identity, makes a passionate case for the justification of abortion in rape cases. The author first told his daughter's story through one of his newspaper columns in 1981. His decision to do so was prompted by a U.S. Senate committee vote to further restrict funds for poor women's abortions, even in cases of rape or incest. The following viewpoint includes the father's original newspaper column and some of his more recent thoughts about his daughter's ordeal.

As you read, consider the following questions:

1. Do you agree with the author's attack on the senators who voted to restrict funding for abortion in rape cases? Why or why not?
2. If you were in the author's position, what would you have done? Why?
3. How did this experience affect the author's opinion concerning the importance of family?

Anonymous, "A Father's Story," from *The Choices We Made*, edited by Angela Bonavoglia. Copyright © 1991 by Angela Bonavoglia. Reprinted by permission of Random House, Inc.

I have been wondering whether to tell you a personal story that seems to me to have general implications. This is one of those sad family stories that normally you don't find fathers talking about in public, or even very much with close friends.

But I picked up the newspaper the other day to read that a Senate committee had voted to abolish payments for abortions for the poor, even when the pregnancies are the result of rape.

Now this was not a question of cutting the budget. Abortion costs for poor women who are raped do not amount to a large sum. Rather it was a question of morality. Republican Senator Jesse Helms of North Carolina, and the Moral Majority which follows him around, are convinced that abortion is wrong even when the woman who wants one wants it because she has been raped. . . .

I object to what the Senate committee did. But I have the human instinct to object even more strenuously when I reason that, by the same standard with which the senators dealt with the poor, they will shortly deal with me.

So let me tell you my story.

A Daughter's Story

A few years ago, my daughter attended an enormous Fourth of July celebration at the Washington Monument. It was a free show with fireworks and flags and entertainment, and, according to the newspaper account, the large crowd behaved well.

But as my daughter strolled alone off the monument grounds and entered a side street, a car rolled up next to the sidewalk. Three men emerged from it, seized her roughly, and, before she could do more than utter a half-stifled cry, put her into the backseat, where two more men held her to the floor.

She was tied, gagged, and taken to a house, the location of which she cannot now identify. She was kept in the house for the rest of the night, during which time she was repeatedly beaten and raped.

The next morning she was blindfolded, driven back to the monument grounds, and shoved out of the car. Eventually, sometime about midday, she made her way home.

During the time she was gone, there was, of course, a great deal of worry and anxiety at that home. And, I must confess, anger. Her arrival was followed by various interviews with policemen who tried to be helpful to a hysterical girl but couldn't be, because the hysterical girl could only estimate the time she had been in the car, describe the inside of a house, and sob out some meaningless first names.

That's really the end of the story. Except, of course, that within a very short time, my daughter knew that she was pregnant.

Now I would like to ask Senator Helms what he would do if he had been the father of the girl. I know what I did. And I can promise the senator and the Moral Majority and all the shrill voices of the right-to-life movement that no matter what law they may pass and how stringent the penalty, I would do it again. . . .

'You've been found guilty of being poor, female and raped, and we sentence you to nine months' hard labor'

Mike Peters. Reprinted with permission of UFS, Inc.

My daughter was in her early twenties at the time. Right after it happened, within a couple of days, we took her to a well-known Washington hospital. People told me later there is something you can do right away that prevents impregnation. I didn't know . . . for a guy who's had a few children, I know less than I should. Anyway, the doctors examined her, but they did not do anything. She came back from the hospital, and within a couple of months, we knew that she was pregnant.

As soon as we knew, there was no question in my mind about what course to take. I didn't have any feelings about murder or innocent life. That's an argument that never went through my head. I never argued with myself or with my wife. We never raised the questions that all the right-to-life ethicists raise. The fetus didn't mean anything to me. I have no love for something that was brought about by horror, terror, and attack.

These senators who have no knowledge or understanding of

what they're talking about and who vote in committee to abolish abortions for poor people, even in cases of rape and incest, I don't think they have any morality. It's Godless, it's cruel, it's insensitive, and it's stupid. They are not seeing the human beings involved. They're not seeing love. They're not seeing affection. They're not seeing goodness of heart. They're not seeing family—they're not seeing the care of a mother and father. They're not seeing anything except some batty feeling that the only thing that matters is the unborn. They have no concern for the born—that is, my daughter, her mother, me.

The Abortion Ended the Trauma

My wife and I took my daughter for the abortion and brought her home. The abortion was not a traumatic experience. It was an end to a traumatic experience.

It passes through your head . . . what if she had had to carry that pregnancy to term? I don't know. Look, I'm only the father of the daughter, but how would you like to live with the constant reminder of what had happened on such and such a day, such and such number of years ago, which represented the very depths of despair and horror and fright? It doesn't seem to me that God intended that a child should remind a mother of horror, fear.

If abortion had been illegal, I would have violated the law, if I could have. I would have done *anything* to prevent her from having to carry that pregnancy to term.

The experience made me realize how important in America, in the whole world, a family is. A family is a unit, an essential unit. It's stronger in your affection, in your idea of what your values are, than your country or your city or your government or your boss or the company you work for. When it gets right down to where you stand, you stand with your family and you want to protect your family. When Senator Helms or any other people want to interfere with your family, and they represent the law, then you have to fight the law.

I suppose that's how revolutions start.

155

> *"Let us not mistakenly think that the sorrow of rape can be erased by the act of ultimate violence, the slaying of an unborn child."*

Rape Does Not Justify Abortion

Mary Monica

In the following viewpoint, the author recounts being assaulted and wounded in an attempted rape. She contemplates what would have happened had she in fact been raped and become pregnant. The author concludes that rape does not justify abortion, because the destruction of an unborn child is far worse than the horror of rape. To protect her identity, the author uses the pseudonym Mary Monica.

As you read, consider the following questions:

1. How did the attempted rape change the author's life?
2. Do you believe that the author would have the same opinion if, in fact, she had been raped? Why or why not?
3. Do you agree with the author that rape does not justify abortion? Why or why not?

Mary Monica, "Abortion in Case of Rape?" *Fidelity,* March 1989. Reprinted with permission.

Some years ago the impossible happened, the nightmare that every decent woman fears. I became the victim of a violent sex offender, a 1987 crime statistic.

Surely I would have regarded myself as least likely to be targeted for such a crime. I had attended an orthodox Catholic school and grew up inspired by the writings of the famous Daniel A. Lord, the champion of purity. At age 12, I had made my own private vow to wed only a Catholic, and to remain a virgin until marriage. My dream? To rear a large family in the tradition of Blessed Anna Maria Taigi, St. Elizabeth Anne Seton, and other famous Catholic wives and mothers.

My ideals were considered an anachronism in the fast-moving era of the new morality. Word travelled quickly in our small town about which girls were not "willing." I soon found myself thoroughly ostracized from the dating game, while I heartbrokenly watched other girls succumb to the lure of the then new birth control pill. When I reached the age of thirty-three with just six dates to my record, I realized that those wedding bells would just never ring for me. And I felt some resentment that the Church, while expounding on the necessity of Catholics marrying only Catholics, of practicing chastity before marriage, of living *Humanae Vitae*, did absolutely nothing to bring together the rare men and women who still believed in these virtues.

Lonely and often depressed, I poured myself into fulfilling a secondary vocation: mothering other people's children. Soon I had devoted hundreds of hours of volunteer work to helping neglected children, and the mentally retarded and handicapped.

Shattered Peace

My serene life exploded into shards that day an unkempt man, armed with a hunting knife, forced his way into my peaceful home, shouting that he was going to kill me. Terror immobilized me when I realized who the stranger was. The entire town had been disturbed when this violent offender, who had brutally and repeatedly raped a frail, elderly widow, had been released from the nearby state prison and relocated right in our quiet neighborhood. And there he was in my living room, eyes burning and mouth leering as he pointed the weapon at me, insisting he was going to murder me if I did not submit to rape.

I remembered St. Maria Goretti, and the long dormant grace of Confirmation steeled my veins. I heard myself declare, "No! Christ will protect me!"

In a frenzied fury, the convict leapt upon me, but due to my determined efforts, found himself unable to rape me. Instead he attempted to murder me. In the life-and-death struggle, I realized we were floundering beneath my picture of the Sacred Heart of Jesus. Quietly I surrendered my life to God and His

157

Virgin Mother, praying for rescue. Moments later, neighbors pounded frantically at my back door. The criminal panicked and fled. Bleeding heavily, I realized that I was still wearing my treasured Miraculous Medal. It was the feast of Mary, Mother of Mercy.

Abortion Is the Greater Evil

The issue of rape and incest must be faced squarely. Public funds should be denied for abortion in these cases because abortion is a great evil, and one that cannot be remedied. There is no second chance for an unborn child who has been dismembered. It is important to remember that a child of rape has not wronged its mother or anyone else.

It *is* unjust that a woman must carry to term a child conceived through rape. Yet it is a greater injustice to kill the child. Rape is a terrible act for many reasons, including brutality, humiliation, and the risk of venereal disease and unwanted pregnancy for the woman. It is also terrible because it risks placing the woman in great temptation to kill.

Mary Meehan, *Human Life Review,* Winter 1990.

My most priceless possession, my virginity, had been miraculously preserved, but not my bodily health. As the ambulance rushed me to the hospital, I began going into shock. I was operated on by one of the best surgeons in the country. The surgery was successful, he later informed me, but the knife wound had completely severed a nerve. He was very sorry, but I would always suffer a certain degree of lifetime handicap, and would probably require major surgery again in a few months. He felt that with daily, intensive physical therapy, I could return to work the next year—with limitations, of course.

"You'll have few limitations," he smiled at me warmly. "You're a fighter."

After he left my private room, I lay numb. The attack had probably only lasted five minutes. My disability would be with me for a lifetime.

What Might Have Happened

As I clenched my teeth in waves of pain, my mind wandered into the realm of *what might have happened.* I recently had become involved with our parish's prolife group, and had even spoken to the pastor about the critical need for natural family planning classes for our young married couples, many of whom were resorting to contraceptives. Having read many books on natural planning, I was very familiar with the signs of female fertility. The day of my attack, I suddenly realized, was my day to ovulate. If the criminal had succeeded in finally raping me, I would have become pregnant.

In my support of right-to-life groups, I had frequently encountered that difficult question, even from practicing Catholics: "But what about pregnancies resulting from rape? Why should a woman be forced to carry her attacker's child?" My pleas on behalf of the baby seemed weak in comparison to the trauma of a desperate girl carrying a rape-conceived child. On the day of my attack I had almost become one of those tragic cases. Really, what would I have done?

Having formerly worked in a hospital, I knew what the emergency room procedure would have been. I would have been offered a drug that would have "prevented pregnancy." Yet I knew these drugs, if taken after ovulation, really prevented the implantation of the already-conceived child in the uterus. I bitterly imagined the opposition I would have encountered if I had refused the abortifacient.

I imagined myself enduring the nine months of an unwanted, high-risk pregnancy, along with the rude and curious stares and malicious whispers from the public. I saw myself enduring labor, not a labor of love and joy, but of grim duty, to deliver a child whom I would have immediately been forced to place for adoption in a distant locale, where its tragic origin would have remained unknown. Indeed, abortion seemed an easy solution in such a situation.

A Silent Scream

Yet even as my own wound screamed with pain, I remembered another scream, a silent one. Just before my attack, I had previewed a video for our prolife group. *Eclipse of Reason* was a grisly film, deftly handled by the ex-abortionist turned prolifer, Dr. Bernard Nathanson. A camera expertly placed within the uterus revealed an ethereal-faced, mid-term infant boy, serenely sucking his thumb. All the details were complete—blond fuzz, eyebrows, miniature fingernails. The little fellow looked no different from the prematures I had observed in the hospital nursery.

After viewing the beautiful activities of the child, blissfully unaware of what was to happen next, the instruments of destruction were inserted into the womb, and the color changed from the pink of an unborn baby to the red of destruction, as the hapless child was torn apart alive. The camera focused on each splintered piece of baby as it was extracted and deposited on a table. At last the crushed head, oozing brain tissue, was pulled out, and the procedure was done.

I shuddered at the memory. At least I had been given anesthesia during my surgery. That child had been given none. If I could scarcely endure the post-operative pain I was suffering now, what had that poor baby felt while its body was cut and mangled? What terror and panic had raced through its little brain before it was crushed forever? Rape was a horrible crime. But the sufferings of rape victims could never equal the death agonies of aborted children conceived out of such unions.

We Must Choose Life

I knew, then, in spite of the pain and emotional turmoil, that the Catholic Church was right when she insisted on the sanctity of human life. And I knew the next time I was asked the question, "Oh yeah, what about rape cases?" I could look the interrogator straight in the eye and say, "You're talking to a woman who was almost one of those cases. I'll never forget the trauma I endured. But that still would not have justified the killing of the blameless baby. If anyone should get capital punishment, it is the rapist, not his child."

What the victims of sexual attack need, regardless of whether or not they become pregnant, is what my community unselfishly gave me: Christian love. Priests and ministers of all denominations hurried to the hospital to console me. Flowers and cards flooded my private room. People who admitted they rarely prayed were now praying for my recovery. And during the long months of healing, volunteers cooked my meals, cleaned my house, changed my splints, purchased my groceries, and drove me to my daily physical therapy. They told me they loved me and listened with compassion when I broke down and cried, for I had much to cry about. I wept for my assailant, who I learned had been born of an incestuous union. A battered and unwanted child, he had been exposed to depravity and pornography at a tender age. I cried for his other victims, many of whom had been too ashamed and terrified to press charges against him. Two victims of his sex attacks, I had been informed, were little girls. I wept for their crushed innocence, that had been destroyed at such a tender age. Why, oh God, why, does our society allow such crimes to continue unchecked?

"Impurity," St. Thomas Aquinas wrote in the thirteenth century, "leads inevitably to violence." Rape is certainly an act of violence. But let us not mistakenly think that the sorrow of rape can be erased by the act of ultimate violence, the slaying of an unborn child. No matter how they are conceived, let the children live.

The Ability to Empathize

Whether abortion is justified when the fetus suffers from a genetic disease, mental retardation, or physical defects is much debated. Many people agree that severe fetal defects indeed justify abortion. They contend that not all families can cope with the enormous demands of raising a severely disabled child. They also argue that the disabled children themselves suffer lives filled with agony.

However, others argue that aborting a severely deformed fetus is a form of selective genocide. It is immoral, according to these critics, to allow only "perfect" children to be born and to kill all those who are disabled, mentally retarded, or otherwise imperfect.

Consider the following viewpoints, which recount the true stories of two women who fully expected that they would deliver severely deformed babies if they carried their pregnancies to term. As you read, try to imagine how each woman felt—in other words, try to empathize with each woman. The ability to empathize, to see life and experience its joys and problems through another person's eyes and feelings, is a helpful skill to acquire if one is to learn from the life situations of others.

Sarah's Story

In graduate school at 26, I worked part-time as a local television reporter and kept up an active social life in between work and classes. I was constantly accused of burning the candle at both ends, a charge that took on merit when I began having irregular menstrual periods that sometimes broke through in the middle of my Pill cycle. After 10 years on the Pill, I figured it was time to take a rest and allow my body to regulate itself naturally. Besides, the fellow student with whom I'd fallen in love was leaving town for the summer. Until he left, we could simply use condoms, I reasoned.

The night before he left town, *the rubber broke,* and I knew instantly I had conceived. . . . In 10 years of sexual activity, I had never had unprotected sex, but suddenly I was faced with the very real possibility of an unwanted and extremely dangerous pregnancy.

My body has a chemical imbalance that leads to wide mood

swings: sometimes euphoria, sometimes depression. However, my illness is completely controllable by the prescription-dispensed medication lithium carbonate—which can cause severe heart defects in fetuses. If I were suddenly to stop taking the medication, I would almost certainly have to be hospitalized and, in the extreme case, probably become suicidal. I've been advised against pregnancy except under well-planned, medically supervised circumstances. . . .

Two weeks later, long enough for me to suspect that I'd actually missed a period, I had a blood serum pregnancy test. . . . The results were negative, and my late period was attributed to my body's trouble readjusting after the Pill. Five weeks or so later, I still hadn't started my period and felt truly awful. . . . After vomiting all morning one Tuesday, I slipped into the university health clinic for a quick examination. I learned I was two months pregnant. . . .

I called in sick to work and drove home, fighting off waves of revulsion. Once inside my apartment, I headed directly to the telephone. My hands trembled as I dialed the number of the abortion clinic. Between sobs, I scheduled my abortion for the following Saturday. I hung up the phone and the dam broke. "No, this can't happen to me!" I screamed as I heaved my purse across the room, scattering the contents all over the floor. I began hurling every object within reach. Finally I sank to the floor and cradled my abdomen. "I'm sorry, baby," I cried. "Mommy's so sorry."

The next day I consulted both an obstetrician and a specialist, looking for *a chance* that my baby could be born normal, but the verdict was the same: if the baby lived, there was a probability it would be deformed; if I stopped taking the medication, I would be hospitalized.

Feeling like the loneliest person in the world, I turned to my best friend for support. To her, the issue was clear: I had no money, no insurance, and no resources to care for a handicapped child. She felt it would be horribly cruel to knowingly bring a sick baby into the world. I agreed with her. . . .

The decision to have an abortion was the most agonizing choice of my life—but the only humane alternative I felt I had.

Reprinted with permission of *Ms.* Magazine © 1989.

Theresa's Story

When she was eight weeks along in her pregnancy—during a critical time for the baby's development—Theresa came down with German measles.

Although this was in early 1970, three years before the U.S. Supreme Court would legalize abortion nationwide, abortion was legally available in California to women who were believed to be carrying severely deformed fetuses.

But Theresa, who had waited until the fifth month of pregnancy before seeking prenatal care, really had no conception of what German measles might mean to her, to her child, or to her future.

"My brother's girlfriend worked for an obstetrician-gynecologist," Theresa says. "I went to see him.". . .

The doctor told Theresa what she could expect should she decide to have the baby, which he strongly advised against. "He told me that last year he had delivered a baby whose mother had come in contact with someone who had German measles.

"The baby was born deaf . . . retarded, with its intestines outside its body. And this woman hadn't even had measles herself. . . . The doctor told me that my baby would be a vegetable, or worse. And he said that if, by some chance, this was not apparent at birth, then by age 5 something devastating would show up."

Theresa left the doctor's office almost in a trance. But she did not waver in her decision to bear her child. Her faith, she says, was in God.

"I knew that baby had a soul," Theresa tells me, looking straight into my eyes, "and I couldn't destroy it.". . .

Today, that baby is a 19-year-old man.

His mother says that not only was he normal—"until he was 5, I just kept *waiting* for something to happen"—but also that his IQ tests show him in the range of 150. . . .

This summer, the man that Theresa calls just one of God's miracles entered the seminary to become a Catholic priest.

After reading these two viewpoints, consider the following questions:

1. Do you think Sarah and Theresa made the right decisions? Why or why not?

2. Imagine yourself facing each decision. What, if anything, would you have done differently? Why?

3. Imagine that you are an opponent of abortion attempting to dissuade Sarah from having an abortion. What arguments would you use to convince her to give birth?

4. Imagine that you are Theresa's doctor attempting to persuade her to have an abortion. What arguments would you use to convince her to terminate her pregnancy?

If you are doing this activity as a member of a class or group, discuss your answers with other class or group members. Listen carefully to the reasons others present for their answers. You may find that your own views have changed after listening to your classmates' opinions.

Periodical Bibliography

The following articles have been selected to supplement the diverse views presented in this chapter.

William F. Buckley Jr. "Abortion and the Rapee," *National Review,* December 8, 1989.

Margaret Carlson "Abortion's Hardest Cases," *Time,* July 9, 1990.

Julie Shaw Cole "Why Abort the Imperfect?" *Utne Reader,* May/June 1990.

Zillah Eisenstein "Fetal Position," *The Nation,* November 20, 1989.

Wanda Franz "The APA, Henry David, and the 'Unwanted Child,'" *National Right to Life News,* October 5, 1989. Available from Suite 500, 419 7th St. NW, Washington, DC 20004.

Glamour "This Is What You Thought: 71 Percent Say It's Not Wrong to Abort a Handicapped Fetus," January 1988.

Perri Klass "The Perfect Baby?" *The New York Times Magazine,* January 29, 1989.

M. Krance "When Prenatal Tests Bring Bad News," *American Health,* July/August 1989.

Mary Meehan "Rape and Abortion: Don't Forget Robin," *Human Life Review,* Winter 1990. Available from 150 E. 35th St., New York, NY 10016.

Sarah Mills "Abortion Under Siege," *Ms.,* July/August 1989.

Terence Monmaney "When Abortion Is Denied: What of the 'Unwanted?'" *Newsweek,* August 22, 1988.

Katha Pollitt "Children of Choice," *The New York Times Magazine,* November 20, 1988.

Anna Quindlen "This Child I Carry," *The New York Times,* May 12, 1988.

Charles E. Rice "Establishment Pro-Life Posturing, " *The New American,* March 12, 1991. Available from 770 Westhill Blvd., Appleton, WI 54915.

J.C. Willke "Assault, Rape, and Abortion: Should We Kill an Innocent Baby for the Crime of His Father?" *National Right to Life News,* April 6, 1989.

Should Abortion
Remain Legal?

Chapter Preface

In 1973, the U.S. Supreme Court legalized abortion nationwide. Many people, particularly women's rights supporters, believed the decision would put an end to dangerous self-induced
and "back alley" abortions performed by unqualified abortionists.
But whether legalized abortion has improved women's health is
still the subject of heated controversy.

"*Roe v. Wade* made abortion safe and legal," writes Angela
Bonavoglia in the introduction to her book *The Choices We
Made*. "Gone were the days of . . . traveling to unknown ad-
dresses in unmarked cars, having 'surgery' without an anes-
thetic, and surrendering to the hands of charlatans and oppor-
tunists." Bonavoglia believes that legal abortion saves women's
lives. She states that of the 1.6 million legal abortions performed
annually in the U.S., only 6 women die from the procedure. In
contrast, approximately the same number of abortions are performed in Mexico, where abortion is illegal, but 140,000 women
die annually from the procedure.

Others argue that legalized abortion has not improved wom-
en's health. David C. Reardon contends in his book *Aborted
Women: Silent No More* that the number of abortions performed
annually in the U.S. since 1973 has risen dramatically. This increase results in a high number of injuries suffered by women.
For example, he says, out of approximately 1 million abortions
performed in 1977, 100,000 complications, such as infection and
excessive bleeding, were reported. As Reardon explains,
"Though the odds of any particular woman suffering ill effects
from an abortion have dropped, the *total* number of women who
suffer and die from abortion is far greater than ever before."

While abortion-related deaths in the U.S. have decreased since
1973, experts disagree on whether legalized abortion has improved women's health overall. The authors in the following
chapter debate this issue and other legal aspects of abortion.

"Reproductive freedom . . . goes to the heart of what this country stands for: to the principles embodied in our Bill of Rights."

Abortion Should Remain Legal

Faye Wattleton

Many people contend that courts should not limit the availability of abortion in any way. In the following viewpoint, Faye Wattleton argues that abortion is a woman's fundamental right that must be legally protected. Wattleton maintains that women's reproductive rights are sacrosanct, and that no government, politician, or court should ever interfere with these rights. Wattleton is president of Planned Parenthood Federation of America, a New York City-based organization that advocates abortion rights.

As you read, consider the following questions:

1. What examples does Wattleton give to show that the U.S. Supreme Court has historically expanded rights not clearly expressed in the Constitution?
2. Why will women inevitably have abortions regardless of laws, in the author's opinion?
3. What should government do in order to reduce the need for abortion, according to Wattleton?

"Reproductive Rights *Are* Fundamental Rights," by Faye Wattleton first appeared in the January/February 1991 issue of *The Humanist* and is reprinted by permission.

Today, the reproductive rights of women are imperiled as never before. In July 1989—16 years after *Roe v. Wade* recognized women's constitutional right to abortion—the Supreme Court retreated from that historic ruling. It cleared the way for laws that victimize poor women seeking abortions. And in two subsequent rulings in June 1990, the court invited restrictions on teenagers' access to abortion.

It's easy to recognize *exactly* what the anti-choice zealots are doing by attacking society's most vulnerable targets—the poor and the young—the anti-choice extremists are chipping away at the reproductive rights of *all* women. Plainly put, the Supreme Court rulings invite state governments to put fetuses first. And radicals in every state are trying to do just that. More than 200 anti-choice bills were introduced in state legislatures between July 1989 and January 1991. . . . Fortunately, the reenergized pro-choice majority has defeated most of them. . . .

Eventually, one of these laws (or a similar one) will bring this battle back to the Supreme Court. . . .

Wresting Control from Women

Historically, we have counted on the Supreme Court to expand rights that were not explicit in the Constitution—rights for women, minorities, children, and the disabled. But today's Reagan-packed courts interpret the Constitution the way fundamentalists interpret the Bible—with a stubborn literalism. If a right wasn't spelled out by that first quill pen, it doesn't exist! In other words, "If you don't see it on the shelf, we don't carry it—and we won't order it!"

Step by horrifying step, our government is commandeering control of our bodies, our reproduction, our most private choices. Unless we act now, this dangerous trend won't stop at abortion. It won't even stop at eliminating contraception. Compulsory pregnancy, forced caesareans, surveillance and detention of pregnant women—these are the chilling, *logical* outcome of laws that reduce women to instruments of the state.

If you think I'm being an alarmist, look at the history of Romania under Nicolae Ceausescu. To boost the birthrate, the dictator banned contraception *and* abortion. Over time, birthrates were virtually unchanged—but the maternal death rate skyrocketed. Nearly 1,000 Romanian women died *each year* from illegal abortions—and those are just the ones who went to hospitals. Countless others, terrified of the law, chose to die at home. Today, in Bucharest alone, up to *30,000* women await hospital treatment for abortion complications. And *40,000* babies have been left orphaned or abandoned. This is the grisly legacy of a state that tried to control its citizens' reproduction. Women are *not* instruments of the state—in Romania, in the

United States, or anywhere else in the world. We are *persons,* with human needs and human rights. Without reproductive autonomy, our other rights are meaningless. Our dignity is destroyed. And the first victims will be those among us who are already most vulnerable, those whose rights are already precarious, those whose access to health care is already limited: the young and the poor. And that usually means minorities.

Fundamental Freedoms

But reproductive freedom is an issue that goes beyond the disadvantaged, beyond state boundaries, and far beyond abortion itself. It goes to the heart of what this country stands for: to the principles embodied in our Bill of Rights. The authors of that great document and its great defenders—such as Daniel Webster, Claude Pepper, and William Brennan—knew that certain fundamental freedoms must be *guaranteed*—insulated from public debate and immune to partisan politics.

Protect Legal Abortion

I am opposed to a repeal of the Supreme Court's decision on *Roe v. Wade.* I am opposed to a constitutional amendment banning abortion. I am opposed to laws that remove what is legal from the reach of some, especially the poor, by saying some medical plans will pay for this legal procedure but some will not. I am opposed to approaching what I believe to be a moral and ethical decision by writing sweeping laws that put every man, woman, child, and developing fetus into one category for judgment. Such legislative action results in indiscriminate denial of the variety of human circumstances and becomes discriminatory intrusion into one of the most private moments of decision in the human life span.

Judith Craig, *Christian Social Action,* April 1990.

For over 200 years, America has been "a light unto the nations." How disgraceful that, as the Berlin Wall came down and the Iron Curtain parted, the only barricade that began to crumble in *this* country was the precious wall protecting our private freedoms!

Those fundamental freedoms are the proudest heritage of our nation. But our heritage of Puritanism also remains deeply rooted. As a nineteenth-century humorist said, "The Puritans fled from a land of despotism to a land of freedom—where they could not only enjoy their own religion but where they could prevent everybody else from enjoying theirs!"

The flames of intolerance still burn brightly in this nation.

And, like all fanatics, *today's* Puritans subscribe to their own moral code—a code that embraces far more brutality than morality. To "save lives," they burn clinics. To "defend womanhood," they taunt and threaten pregnant women. To "strengthen the family," they invade our privacy. Blinded by their disregard for the neediest of women, they insist that making abortion harder to get will make it go away.

Basic Rights Attacked

Haven't these zealots learned *anything* from history? Throughout time, women with unwanted pregnancies have always ended them, regardless of the law, regardless of the risk to their lives. Throughout the world, women *and* men equate freedom and democracy with the right to make private reproductive decisions free from government intrusion!

Again, Romania provides a perfect example. When Ceaucescu was overthrown, two of the first acts of the new government were to decriminalize abortion and to deregulate the private ownership of typewriters. The new regime clearly recognized that reproductive choice is as *fundamental* as freedom of speech.

If only our own government were so wise. On the contrary, President Bush has taken a jackhammer to the bedrock of our basic rights. He has repeatedly asked the Supreme Court to overturn *Roe v. Wade*. He has attacked the federal family planning program, which helps *prevent* half a million abortions each year. And in a Supreme Court brief, his administration attacked not only the right to abortion but the very concept of privacy that underlies our right to contraception!

It's nothing short of obscene that women are forced to expose themselves to politicians—to submit our private matters, our private decisions, and our private parts to *public* debate! Surely, America's politicians have more important things to do—like house the homeless, feed the hungry, and educate the ignorant. Like tackle the root cause of the abortion issue: unintended pregnancy.

Hands-Off Government Needed

Instead of compulsory ignorance, we need comprehensive education on human sexuality—in every home and in every school, from kindergarten through twelfth grade. Instead of laws that punish pregnant women, we need our government's commitment to develop better birth control. Instead of pontifications about the unborn, we need proper care for the children already born.

Finally, instead of state control of our reproduction, we need to be left alone by the government. We need to remove the abortion issue *forever* from the legislative arena. *We need a universal recognition that our civil liberties are off limits to partisan debate!*

Our advocacy is vital to making these ideals a reality. Every one of us can and *must* make a difference. We must start at home, talking openly and often with our children about sexuality. We must activate our communities, promoting comprehensive sexuality education in local schools. We must activate our colleagues and return reproductive rights to their proper context. These are profound ethical, religious, and philosophical questions—to be debated and decided by individuals and families, *never* by politicians.

Finally, we must activate our elected officials—write to them, call them, lobby them. Tell them to stay out of our bedrooms and out of our family affairs! Tell them again and again that our reproductive rights are fundamental rights! Indivisible rights! *Nonnegotiable* rights!

"Society must take a stand through the law that killing is wrong."

Abortion Should Be Illegal

Nancy E. Meyers

According to the National Research Council in Washington, D.C., approximately 1.5 million abortions are performed annually in the U.S. Many Americans who believe this number is much too high advocate legislation restricting or prohibiting abortion. In the following viewpoint, Nancy E. Meyers agrees with this view. Because she believes abortion is murder and a violation of human rights, Meyers argues that abortion should be illegal. Meyers is the media relations director of the National Right to Life Committee, a Washington, D.C.-based group that opposes abortion.

As you read, consider the following questions:

1. In Meyers's view, why are legal restrictions on personal choice necessary in society?
2. According to the author, how does a lack of knowledge of the medical facts affect a woman's abortion decision?
3. Do you agree with Meyers that abortion is as immoral as slavery? Why or why not?

Nancy E. Meyers, "Abortion Is Morally Wrong." This article appeared in the October 1989 issue and is reprinted with permission from *The World and I,* a publication of The Washington Times Corporation, copyright © 1989.

Abortion is becoming the great moral issue of this century, much as slavery was in the last. The July 1989 Supreme Court decision in *Webster v. Reproductive Health Services* marked a new stage in the debate because, for the first time in 16 years, the American people were given back at least limited power to protect unborn life, and pending court cases may give back even more.

Media attention has begun to focus on strategies and politics in the abortion debate—how the proabortion and prolife activists work, how the issue will play in elections, and how lawmakers will work to pass or block protective legislation.

The proabortion side, especially, is attracting media attention by talk of strategy, activism, and increased momentum on the issue. They talk about choices, politics, personalities, and framing the debate properly. They talk about anything except the central issue before our country—abortion.

The highly motivated prolife movement, meanwhile, continues its activities of education about abortion, lobbying, and public affairs to bring about meaningful protection for all human life. The talk, as it has been since 1973, is about abortion.

Freedom of Choice Is Not Absolute

The current strategy of abortion advocates is to frame the debate in terms of "choice." They ask, who should decide whether a woman may have an abortion—the woman or society at large? Freedom of personal, private choice, they assert, should be absolute in a free country, regardless of reason, timing, or the opinions of others. Society at large should not impose its views on individuals.

The argument is seductive, both because it appeals to the American sense of individuality and because it allows us to not have to wrestle with the moral and philosophical complexity of abortion. The argument for choice allows people to abdicate responsibility; that is, to express discomfort and moral misgivings about abortion while at the same time dismissing the entire argument.

But unqualified free choice, especially in life-and-death issues, does not exist. Despite our many freedoms in the United States, restrictions are in place to protect the vulnerable and to assure a reasonably orderly society. For instance, society does not give a man the choice whether he may rape or beat his wife, though these acts may occur in privacy. Society does not sanction the choice, because rape and beating are wrong.

The plain fact is, our choices are limited by our interdependency and our mutual rights. Simply put: my freedoms stop where your rights begin. A woman's freedom over her own body stops where another body, another life, begins—the life of her child.)

Choice also implicitly requires an informed decision-making process, with knowledge of all the facts and the options. Yet those who advocate abortion protest vehemently against informed consent legislation, which would require a woman to know exactly what is involved in abortion. They argue that to give a woman information about the developing life within her and the procedure involved clouds the decision-making process.

Certainly, facts such as that babies have beating hearts at 18 days, have brain waves at 40 days, and suck their thumbs at six weeks might have the effect of dissuading a woman from choosing to destroy that life. Surely, the knowledge that in early abortions a suction machine many times more powerful than the household vacuum pulls apart a developing child limb from limb and sucks her out into an unrecognizable mass of pulp is unsettling. So is the fact of how most later abortions are performed. Later abortions—second trimester and afterward—require the abortionist to dismember the fetus, which is too large to get through the cervix, and pull the pieces out of the womb with a pliers-like instrument, then put the baby back together to ensure no body parts remain in the uterus to cause infection.

But what reasonable argument can there be to deliberately withhold undisputed medical facts from women? When does the plain truth prevent a conscious, careful choice? How does more information in any way diminish the ability to decide? Clearly, the proabortion side wants to keep people in the dark, to withhold the very medical information that is critical to an informed, rational decision, because they advocate abortion—at any stage and for any reason—as the best alternative. Many women now active in the prolife movement suffered greatly after having abortions and discovering, sometimes years later, what the procedure involved and how unborn children develop and grow. These women now speak out actively for informed consent so that other women will understand the "choice" involved in every abortion: life or death.

An Undeniable Humanity

Medicine and technology are advancing more quickly than ever thought possible, and these scientific developments compel us to recognize the undeniable humanity of all people, regardless of age, race, or status in society. Proud parents can show sonograms of babies at six weeks to friends and family. Doctors are able to diagnose and treat children in the womb for a variety of conditions. Medical advances are helping younger babies to survive, making the point of viability earlier than ever dreamed possible. Babies born at 20 and 21 weeks have survived, and close to one-third of babies born at 24 weeks survive. Yet abortions are performed throughout the entire stage of pregnancy.

With our ever-increasing knowledge about the undeniable humanity of unborn babies, the concept of "choosing" to kill these children at will becomes increasingly indefensible. So we must offer protection for those who cannot speak for themselves.

The Silent Voices

There are those whom we do not hear, since they cannot speak for themselves. Justice and morality cry out that we must speak for them. No one else will.

Nackey Loeb for *The Union Leader,* reprinted with permission.

Ultimately, this is not a debate about whether a woman has a right to choose to get her ears pierced, or to have an appendectomy or hysterectomy. We are talking about the decision whether to take a human life, which currently happens more than 4,000 times a day in the United States, 1.5 million times a year.

The American people instinctively know this and are deeply uncomfortable with those abortions that occur for social reasons. If abortion were just another surgical procedure, people would not have such misgivings about it.

Society Must Take a Stand

Polls consistently show Americans oppose the alarming frequency and the accessibility of abortion. Americans are shocked to learn that 40 percent of all abortions—640,000 each year —are second, third, and fourth abortions. Most people are decidedly against abortion as a means of birth control, yet half of all women getting abortions admit neither they nor their partner used any form of birth control.

The prolife movement exists because abortion is not just a political position or a choice, but a life-and-death moral issue. Abortion will continue unabated unless human rights activists stand up for the less powerful in our society and demand rights. Even though some abortions will still occur, just as child abuse, murder, and bigotry are still with us, society must take a stand through the law that killing is wrong. Eventually, the views and laws of society will pass by the minority of people who view abortion as a "positive good," just as the laws and society against discrimination have passed by people with remnants of racism.

Activists in the prolife movement, after years of struggle to end abortion, know that ensuring all Americans have a right to life and freedom, and convincing society at large that protection of all human life is crucial to our future as a nation, will not happen overnight. But the prolife movement has been going strong for years without any real power to protect unborn children, and will continue as more rights are granted.

As Wrong as Slavery

Abraham Lincoln's Second Inaugural Address, which he gave as the Civil War raged, spoke of the great moral and physical struggle tearing apart the United States at the time; Lincoln foreshadowed the equally divisive moral struggle we face today.

He said: "Both read the same Bible and pray to the same God, and each invokes His name against the other. It may seem strange that any men should dare risk a just God's assistance in wringing their bread from the sweat of other men's faces, but let us judge not, that we not be judged."

Lincoln acknowledged that apparently sincere, well-meaning people stood on both sides of the slavery issue, but he expressed what we know today to be the truth. For despite all the self-serving arguments of the slave owners or the economic arguments against dismantling an entrenched social structure, slavery was always deeply wrong and ever at odds with the immediate and ultimate goals of a free nation. Slavery was no less intrinsically wrong when it was legal and widespread than it is to us today.

And so it is with abortion. Killing another human being wantonly and at will is, has always been, and will always be wrong. And yet we live in a country in which 1.5 million unborn children a year are killed without restriction.

Abortion Cannot Be Tolerated

Lincoln's incredulity at the justification of the proslavery forces mirrors that of the prolife movement. We find it hard to understand how the proabortion people, who dare to speak for women's health and lives, can advocate something so destructive as abortion. (And especially, as a woman I am incredulous that so-called feminists advocate abortion as freedom for women when that freedom comes at the expense of another human being's life, many times a female life.) The arguments of the proabortion side ring false when examined against the fundamental rights we cherish so much in our society, much as the arguments for slavery seem shocking and untenable to us today.

Science is on our side. History is on our side. The hearts of Americans, who instinctively respect and cherish all human life, despite race, age, or status, are on our side. Undoubtedly, future generations will look on these years of unrestricted abortion as a temporary setback in the ongoing struggle for freedom for all people.

And so we remain confident, because beyond the raging debate and the shouted slogans and sound bites, beyond the fallacy of choice and the innocent lives taken every year, a quiet but undeniably greater truth exists: Abortion is wrong and cannot be tolerated by a truly free people and a genuinely free nation.

"Access to safe, funded abortion is a positive social need *for all women of childbearing age."*

Legal Abortion Strengthens Women's Rights

Rosalind Pollack Petchesky

Rosalind Pollack Petchesky is director of the Women's Studies Program and professor of political science at Hunter College, City University of New York. In the following viewpoint, Petchesky defends abortion as crucial to women's freedom and equality with men. She deplores the way many feminists apologize for abortion and describe it as a necessary evil. Instead, Petchesky asserts that feminists should emphasize the benefits of abortion to women's well-being. She also argues that a complete social, economic, and cultural revolution is necessary to create real choice for both women and men in matters of sexuality and childbearing.

As you read, consider the following questions:

1. What does the author mean when she argues that abortion is both minimal and indispensable?
2. According to the author, how did the U.S. Supreme Court decision in *Roe v Wade* affect women?
3. What changes does Petchesky specifically advocate to create genuine reproductive freedom in society?

From *Abortion and Woman's Choice: The State, Sexuality, and Reproductive Freedom* (Revised Edition) by Rosalind Pollack Petchesky. Copyright © 1984, 1990 by Rosalind P. Petchesky. Reprinted with the permission of Northeastern University Press, Boston.

Abortion in itself does not create reproductive freedom. It only makes the burdensome and fatalistic aspects of women's responsibility for pregnancy less total. It does not socialize that responsibility, empower a woman in her relations with men or society, or assure her of a liberated sexuality. It only allows her the space to move from one point in her life to the next, if she is a heterosexual woman; to navigate some of the more oppressive patriarchal and institutional forces that are beyond her control. Abortion is but one of many social conditions that encompass women's education, employment, health, reproductive choice, and economic and sexual self-determination. As such, it is both minimal and indispensable.

Yet, since the late 1970s, a negative view of abortion seems to have penetrated feminist thinking as well as the dominant culture. Typically, it takes this form: "Of course, nobody likes abortion; we just think there should be a choice." Sometimes this defensiveness grows out of a pragmatic concern to win a broad base of support. Even committed feminists in the movement for reproductive rights lament that abortion is "a hard issue to organize people about," one that fails to uplift people's spirits or generate joyful, proud symbols (the coathanger is seen as a "last resort"). Sometimes feminist ideas themselves absorb and reflect cultural forces that project abortion as a "necessary evil." Thus Adrienne Rich wrote in the mid-1970s: "No free woman, with 100 percent effective, nonharmful birth control readily available, would 'choose' abortion"; and "abortion is violence: a deep, desperate violence inflicted by a woman upon, first of all, herself."

Blaming the Victim

The basis of this victimizing, victim-blaming position is a perspective that reduces women's condition universally to "male violence." It is also a strain of feminist tradition that idealizes motherhood, implying that the termination of every unwanted pregnancy is somehow a tragedy. Whatever its intention, this view does not accord with the facts. Many, perhaps most, abortions performed today (and, as far as we can tell, through much of history) are not the product of "grim, driven desperation," as Rich calls it, but of women's sober determination to take hold of their lives and, sometimes, of a sense of enlarged power for being able to do so. That abortion may be painful or unpleasant does not make it "violence against oneself" any more than a painful divorce or a mastectomy is "violence against oneself.". . .

The view of abortion as a necessary evil born out of desperate circumstances is a liberal accommodation to recent waves of antiabortion (and antifeminist) ideology. It is a clearly mistaken view, since the conditions underlying rising abortion rates in the 1970s and 1980s have on the whole involved a greater expansion of women's relative power in American society than at any other time. Indeed, historical material seems to suggest a rough hypothesis: The easing of women's access to birth control and abortion (which are positively related) coincides with periods of their increased social power and status; while restrictions on that access usually indicate a broad-scale attack on women's sexual and social autonomy and on feminist movements. Our unnecessarily high rate of abortions in the U.S. relative to other so-called developed countries results not from feminism but from residual conservative influences in the society—influences that inhibit the institutionalization and cultural and moral acceptance of young women as birth control users, and, thus, sexual actors.

Don't Be Afraid to Speak of Abortion

Women who have abortions seldom speak of them. If they do, they must be properly grieved. They must show repentance: "I hated to do it," "I was depressed for months afterwards," "I would never do it again." The social climate dictates that they must act as if they have done something reprehensible, that guilt must follow. Instead, I venture that most women are relieved that they have spared themselves, their families, and society the consequences of an unwanted pregnancy. . . .

We must stop leaning over backwards in order not to offend militant anti-abortion radicals. We must create a climate in which people are not afraid to say, "Yes, I had an abortion. Yes, I perform abortions. Yes, you need an abortion. Yes, I want an abortion." Abortions must become just one of many medical procedures.

Cleo Kocol, *The Humanist*, May/June 1988.

The "necessary evil" concept oddly forgets the spirit of buoyancy infusing not only feminists but masses of women after *Roe v. Wade*. Suddenly the years of terror, of silently fearing pregnancy, of sneaking off to possible sterility or death, and of sex ridden with shame were with a few judicial words going to end. It was a naive faith, for the last several years have shown that deep-rooted ideology and noncompliant administrative and clinical practices were too powerful for a Supreme Court ruling to reverse. The buoyancy was there nonetheless because abortion—easily available, cheap, administered under safe, hygienic conditions early in a pregnancy and in an ambience free of stigma and guilt—*is* a component (not just a condition) of women's liberation. What makes abortion "awful" is the shame and guilt caused by two heavily ideological notions that all women in the society still learn to some degree: (1) the association of fetus with "baby" and the aborting woman with "bad mother," and (2) the assumption that sex for pleasure is "wrong" (for women) and that women who indulge in it have to pay a price. . . .

Don't Apologize for Abortion

Rather than apologize for abortion, feminists must proclaim loudly—as they did in the late 1960s and early 1970s—that access to safe, funded abortion is a *positive social need* for all women of childbearing age. Abortion is a necessary, though far from sufficient, condition of women's essential right and need, not only for bodily health and self-determination, but also for control over their work, their sexuality, and their relations with others—including existing children. From this perspective, abortion conducted under safe, affordable, and stigma-free conditions is neither a necessary evil nor a matter of private choice. Rather, it is a positive benefit that society has an obligation to provide to all who seek it, just as it provides education and health benefits. Put another way, abortion is not simply an "individual right" (civil liberty) or even a "welfare right" (for those "in need") but a "social right."

What does it mean to talk about abortion as a social right or, more accurately, a social need? First, it means that *access* to abortion (as distinct from the actual experience) is necessary to women's well-being and self-determination; therefore, it is closer to a "necessary good" than a "necessary evil," whatever discomfort it may entail. The farther a society moves toward transforming the oppressive socioeconomic and cultural conditions that encumber the meaning/experience of abortion, the more will abortion become a genuine tool of freedom rather than an occasion of misery. In this regard, it is similar to work or divorce. Second, it means that the need for abortion is universal in the sense that its availability is essential to *all* women, for it defines the terms and conditions of "womanhood" in the society; and it is specific in the sense that the need grows out of a particular set of problems. Access to safe, legal abortion is a very different kind of need depending on whether a woman is a fifteen-year-old high school student, a single working woman trying to raise one or two children already, a black woman suffering from hypertension or diabetes, or a recent immigrant trying to get an economic foothold in the U.S. Finally, it means embedding the right to abortion in a much broader array of health, social welfare, and sexual needs. . . .

Creating equality of conditions for reproductive choice means, first, a wide range of social supports that will make having and raising children, or not doing so, a real alternative for *all* people: high-quality, publicly funded health, maternal, and child care; the elimination of reproductively hazardous environments; and the provision of adequate jobs, incomes, housing, and education. Above all, changes in the social arrangements of child care and reproductive decision making will have to be accompanied by basic changes in the sexual division of labor in the economy and the state. As long as women work in segregated jobs, for low pay and with subordinate status, and must bear primary responsibility for children, there can be no "equality" in reproduction. Finally, the meaning of "reproductive rights" must include the full range of treatment services for women with HIV [the AIDS virus] and women on drugs and respect for their reproductive choices. . . .

Second, the conditions of reproductive freedom will have to include cultural as well as socioeconomic changes, specifically changes in the social and sexual relations of reproduction. "Maternal practices" will have to become contributions that men as well as women not only value but achieve. Such changes go way beyond legal reforms such as parental leave benefits, flex-time, child-care centers staffed by men and women, and the like. They require a revolutionary commitment to a cultural revolution that will take hold of families, schools, the media, and ordinary ways of life, even among those in power. The meanings of sex as well as gender will be called into play in such a revolution. Not only the standards of nurturance and who shall provide it are at stake but the socially sanctioned expressions of desire. . . .

Within such a culturally and socially transformed setting, reproductive choices will still occur within institutional frameworks. These institutions—above all, the health-care system—must also undergo sweeping and specific changes before reproductive freedom for all women can exist. . . .

The abortion experience of the past hundred years confirms that realizing the right to abortion requires putting an end to privatized, class-divided medicine and socializing medical care. This will mean, first, that health needs become one essential ground for abortion and that medical personnel who fail to provide essential services will be publicly called to account. Second, it will mean that, rather than twist abortion into the restrictive framework of pathology and cure, we will broaden the dominant meanings of "medical" (and consequently standards of reimbursement) to include *all* aspects of health—preventive, reproductive, and socioeconomic as well as remedial. This expansive approach to a concept of reproductive health will affect public and private financing not only of abortion but of contraception, pregnancy, and prenatal and child care.

"Of all the things which are done to women to fit them into a society dominated by men, abortion is the most violent invasion of their physical and psychic integrity."

Legal Abortion Exploits Women

Daphne de Jong

Daphne de Jong is the former president of Feminists for Life of New Zealand. In the following viewpoint, de Jong claims that legal abortion has destroyed, rather than promoted, women's rights. Instead of demanding the right to destroy their unborn babies, women should fight for the right to have those babies. Only when women insist that their essential role as mothers be recognized both in their private lives and in the workplace, will they achieve full equality, de Jong concludes.

As you read, consider the following questions:

1. What reasons does the author give for her argument that legal abortion manipulates and degrades women?
2. How does de Jong criticize the idea that abortion is a necessity?
3. How does abortion infringe on the rights of others, according to the author?

Daphne de Jong, "The Feminist Sell-Out," *New Zealand Listener,* January 14, 1976. Reprinted with permission.

The women's movement suffers from three classic defense mechanisms associated with minority group status: self-rejection, identification with the dominant group, and displacement.

The demand for abortion at will is a symptom of group self-hatred and total rejection, not of sex *role* but of sex identity.

The womb is not the be-all and end-all of a woman's existence. But it is the physical centre of her sexual identity, which is an important aspect of her self-image and personality. To reject its function, or to regard it as a handicap, a danger or a nuisance, is to reject a vital part of her own personhood. Every woman need not be a mother, but unless every woman can identify with the potential motherhood of all women, no equality is possible. American Negroes gained nothing by straightening their kinky hair and aping the white middle class. Equality began to become a reality only when they insisted on acceptance of their different qualities—"Black is Beautiful."

Pregnant Peoples' Rights

Women will gain their rights only when they demand recognition of the fact that they are people who become pregnant and give birth—and not always at infallibly convenient times—and that pregnant people have the same rights as others.

To say that in order to be equal with men it must be possible for a pregnant woman to become unpregnant at will, is to say that being a woman precludes her from being a fully functioning person. It concedes the point to those who claim that women who want equality really want to be imitation men.

If women must submit to abortion to preserve their lifestyle or career, their economic or social status, they are pandering to a system devised and run by men for male convenience. The politics of sexism are perpetuated by accommodating to expediential societal structures which decree that pregnancy is incompatible with other activities, and that children are the sole responsibility of their mother.

The demand for abortion is a sell-out to male values and a capitulation to male lifestyles rather than a radical attempt to renegotiate the terms by which women and men can live in the world as people with equal rights and equal opportunities. Black "Uncle Toms" have their counterparts not only in women who cling to the chains of their kitchen sinks, but also in those who proclaim their own liberation while failing to recognize that they have merely adopted the standards of the oppressor, and fashioned themselves in his image.

Oppressed groups traditionally turn their frustrated vengeance on those even weaker than themselves. The unborn is the natural scapegoat for the repressed anger and hostility of women, which is denied in traditional male-female relationships, and ridiculed when it manifests itself in feminist protest. Even while proclaiming "her" rights over the fetus, much liberationist rhetoric identifies pregnancy with male chauvinist "ownership." The inference is that by implanting "his" seed, the man establishes some claim over a woman's body ("Keeping her barefoot and pregnant"). Abortion is almost consciously seen as "getting back at" the male. The truth may well be that the liberationist sees the fetus not as a part of her body but as a part of his.

Abortion Manipulates Women

What escapes most liberationist writers is that legal abortion is neither a remedy nor an atonement for male exploitation of women. It is merely another way in which women are manipulated and degraded for male convenience and male profit. This becomes blatantly obvious in the private abortion industries of both Britain and America, and the support given to the proabortion lobby by such exploitative corporations as the *Playboy* empire.

Of all the things which are done to women to fit them into a society dominated by men, abortion is the most violent invasion of their physical and psychic integrity. It is a deeper and more destructive assault than rape, the culminating act of womb-envy and woman-hatred by the jealous male who resents the creative power of women.

Feminists Should Oppose Abortion

For over a hundred years feminists have warned us that abortion is a form of violence and oppression against women and their children. They called it "child-murder" (Susan B. Anthony), "degrading to women" (Elizabeth Cady Stanton), "appalling" proof of "the misery of the working class" (Emma Goldman), "most barbaric" (Margaret Sanger), and "a disowning of feminine values" (Simone de Beauvoir). How have we lost this wisdom? . . .

Abortion advocacy has been poisonous to some of the deeper values of feminism. For example, the need to discredit the fetus has led to the use of terms that would be disastrous if applied to women. "It's so small," "It's unwanted," "It might be disabled," "It might be abused." Too often women are small, unwanted, disabled, or abused. Do we really want to say that these factors erase personhood?

Frederica Mathewes-Green, *Sisterlife*, Winter 1990.

Just as the rapist claims to be "giving women what they want," the abortionist affirms his right to provide a service for which there is a feminine demand.

Offered the quick expedient of abortion, instead of community support to allow her to experience pregnancy and birth and parenthood with dignity and without surrendering her rights as a person, woman is again the victim, and again a willing participant in her own destruction.

The way to equality is not to force women into molds designed for men, but to re-examine our basic assumptions about men and women, about child-care and employment, about families and society, and design new and more flexible modes for living. Accepting short-term solutions like abortion only delays the implementation of real reforms like decent maternity and paternity leaves, job protection, high quality child-care, community responsibility for dependent people of all ages, and recognition of the economic contribution of child-minders. Agitation for the imaginative use of glide time, shared jobs, shorter working weeks, good creches, part-time education and job training, is more constructive for women—and men—torn between career and children, than agitation for abortion.

Women Processed Through Abortion Mills

Today's women's movement remains rooted in 19th-century thinking, blindly accepting patriarchal systems as though they rested on some immutable natural law; processing women through abortion mills to manufacture instant imitation men who will fit into a society made by and for wombless people. Accepting the "necessity" of abortion is accepting that pregnant women and mothers are unable to function as persons in this society. It indicates a willingness to adjust to the status quo which is a betrayal of the feminist cause, a loss of the revolutionary vision of a world fit for *people* to live in. . . .

Human rights are not exclusive. Any claim to a superior or exceptional right inevitably infringes on the rights of someone else. To ignore the rights of others in an effort to assert our own is to compound injustice, rather than reduce it.

"The legalization of abortion brought with it a dramatic decrease in the total number of abortion-related deaths."

Legal Abortion Has Improved Women's Health

Rachel Benson Gold

Legalized abortion has reduced the number of pregnancy-related deaths and injuries in the U.S. and many other countries. In the following viewpoint, Rachel Benson Gold contends that the risk of death or injury from abortion has dropped significantly since the practice was legalized nationwide in 1973. Gold cites evidence showing a complication rate of 0.5 percent for women having legal abortions in 1988. Gold is a senior associate for policy analysis at the Alan Guttmacher Institute, a family-planning research organization in Washington, D.C.

As you read, consider the following questions:

1. How has legal abortion reduced the number of babies born with birth defects, according to Gold?
2. Under what conditions does the author say abortion is safest?
3. According to Gold, what is the likelihood of a legal abortion causing a woman's death?

Excerpted, with permission, from *Abortion and Women's Health* by Rachel Benson Gold. New York: Alan Guttmacher Institute, 1990.

The legalization of abortion brought with it a dramatic decrease in the total number of abortion-related deaths. In 1965, when abortion was still illegal nationwide except in cases of life endangerment, a minimum of 193 women died from illegal abortions, and illegal abortion accounted for nearly 17 percent of all deaths due to pregnancy and childbirth in that year. Fifty-five percent of the abortion-related deaths reported in 1965 were among nonwhite women. Since many deaths from illegal abortion were attributed to other causes on the death certificates or were never reported, the actual number was undoubtedly higher. Even in 1972, when abortion was legal in some states, the Center for Disease Control reported that 41 women died from illegal procedures. Deaths from illegal abortion fell to 22 in 1973, and to seven in 1974—a more than 80 percent decrease between 1972 and 1974. The nationwide legalization of abortion in 1973 replaced almost all illegal procedures with legal abortions by about 1975; however, some women—often those of low income—still resort to illegal procedures.

Abortion-related Deaths Rare

Although deaths from legal abortion are extremely rare, legal abortion—like any surgical procedure entails some risk. As the number of legal abortions rose sharply with legalization in the early 1970s, the number of deaths reported as having resulted from legal abortion also increased temporarily. However, as physicians became more experienced and skilled at performing abortions, the risk of dying from an abortion decreased sharply, and the number of deaths dropped even as the number of legal abortions increased. In 1973, the risk of dying from an abortion was 3.4 deaths per 100,000 legal abortions. This rate fell to 1.3 by 1977. By 1985 the risk of dying from a legal abortion had decreased dramatically—to 0.4 deaths per 100,000 legal abortions.

Six of the 1.6 million women having a legal abortion in 1985 are known to have died. One additional woman reportedly died from an illegal abortion that year, for a total of seven abortion-related deaths. In 1985, abortion, both legal and illegal, accounted for, at most, three percent of all reported pregnancy-related deaths.

Although deaths from either abortion or childbirth are rare, for the period 1981-1985, a woman giving birth was 11 times more likely to die than was a woman having an abortion; the risk of death from childbirth was 6.6 per 100,000 births, compared with an abortion (legal and illegal) death rate of 0.6 per 100,000 abortion procedures.

To put the risk of death from an abortion into further perspective, between 1954 and 1969 the risk of death from a penicillin injection was 1.1 deaths per 100,000 patients receiving an injection. There are no recent data from the United States on the risk of a penicillin injection, but since that time, the risk of death from abortion has fallen considerably.

Some Abortions Are Riskier

Despite the improvements in the safety of legal abortion, some abortions carry more risk than others.

The timing of the abortion is one of the most important factors influencing the risk to the woman. More than half of all abortions are performed at or before eight weeks of pregnancy, when the procedure is the safest. The death rate from an abortion performed at or before eight weeks of pregnancy is 0.2 deaths per 100,000 procedures. The risk rises as gestational age increases. Abortions performed at 11 or 12 weeks of pregnancy are three times more dangerous for the woman than abortions performed at or before eight weeks, although the rate of death from an abortion at 11 or 12 weeks was only 0.6 per 100,000 procedures during 1981-1985.

Abortions performed after the first trimester involve greater

---

Safety of Legal Abortion

Since legalization, women have benefitted from significant advances in medical technology and greater access to high quality services.

Women rarely die from legal abortions. According to the most recent statistics available, only 1 of 200,000 women who have legal abortions die. That is one seventh the number of women who die from childbirth and a tiny fraction of the number of women who used to die from illegal abortions.

National Abortion Federation Fact Sheet, April 1990.

---

risk than do first-trimester procedures. The nine percent of abortions performed in the second trimester accounted for 53 percent of all abortion deaths in 1981-1985.

Different abortion methods are associated with different risks, largely because they are used at different stages of pregnancy. Most first-trimester abortions—and therefore most abortions in the United States are performed using vacuum aspiration, the method that carries the least risk. Techniques used for later abortions, such as medical induction of labor, are associated with higher risks.

The type of anesthesia used also affects the risk facing the woman, with general anesthesia being more dangerous than local anesthesia. Women with preexisting conditions, those who wish to be sterilized at the same time they have an abortion and those having a later abortion are more likely to have general anesthesia. However, even when such factors are controlled for, the risk of anesthesia-related death is higher for abortions performed under general anesthesia (0.37 deaths per 100,000 abortions) than for those performed using local anesthesia (0.15 deaths per 100,000 abortions).

Clinics are as safe as hospitals for abortions performed during the first trimester or early in the second trimester of pregnancy. Similarly, a woman's age does not appear to make a major difference in the risk she faces from an abortion. Perhaps because of differences in income and overall health status in our population, women who are black or are members of other minority groups face a greater risk than do white women.

Decrease in Complications

Like patients undergoing any surgical procedure or women going through childbirth, women having an abortion are at risk of developing complications. Problems range from minor to potentially life-threatening ones. Major complications from abortion may be defined as those that result in pelvic infection with a fever of 100.4°F for three or more days, major surgery, or hemorrhage requiring blood transfusion.

The risk of developing major complications from legal abortion has decreased greatly since 1970. According to the largest study of abortion-related complications, among patients in 1970-1971—when abortion was legal in some states—the rate of major complications was 0.8 per 100 abortion patients who did not have preexisting conditions or undergo concurrent sterilization; by 1975-1978, when abortion was legal nationwide, the risk had decreased to 0.5 per 100. Statistics compiled by the National Abortion Federation for 1988 depict the incidence of complications among abortion patients who received follow-up care from the abortion provider. According to these data, uterine perforations occurred in 0.1 out of every 100 patients. Fewer than 0.2 patients per 100 needed intravenous antibiotics for infections arising from abortion. In total, only 0.5 per 100 patients needed hospitalization because of an abortion complication. The most frequent complication arising from an abortion is an incomplete procedure, requiring the abortion to be performed again; this occurs most often because the fetus or embryo is so small it is missed during an early abortion. Like the risk of mortality, the risk of developing complications is related to when in pregnancy an abortion occurs, as well as to the method and type of anesthesia used. For abortions performed at seven or eight weeks of pregnancy, the risk of developing major complications is almost 0.2 per 100. At 13 or 14 weeks, the risk of developing major complications is about 0.6 per 100. At more than 20 weeks, 1.5 per 100 patients develop major complications.

Deaths from Abortion Before and After Legalization

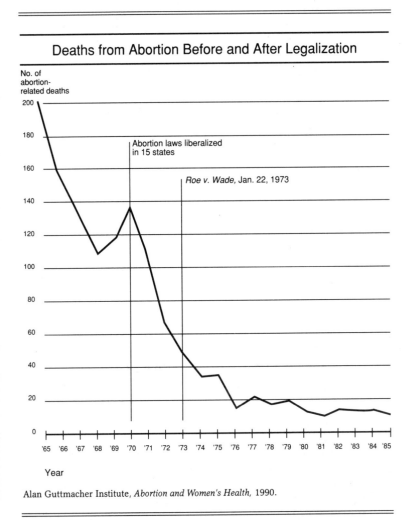

No. of abortion-related deaths

Abortion laws liberalized in 15 states

Roe v. Wade, Jan. 22, 1973

Year

Alan Guttmacher Institute, *Abortion and Women's Health,* 1990.

The risk of developing major complications is also related to the abortion method used, although it is not known precisely how much of the increased risk is due to the different methods that are used at different gestational ages and how much of it is associated with gestational age. Vacuum aspiration, the most common abortion method and the one used early in gestation, has a major complication rate of 0.2 per 100 procedures. D&E

[dilation and evacuation], which is used during the second trimester, has a complication rate of 0.7 per 100 procedures. Labor induction procedures, which are used later in gestation, have the highest risk. As noted above, general anesthesia carries a greater risk than does local anesthesia.

Women giving birth are 100 times more likely than women having abortions to need major abdominal surgery to manage complications. Teenagers do not appear to run a higher risk of developing serious complications of abortion than do older women. . . .

Abortion-related Deaths Reduced

The availability of safe abortion services has been associated with declines in maternal mortality. Maternal mortality in New York State fell by 26 percent in the years immediately following the state's legalization of abortion in 1970. In contrast, maternal mortality fell by only 16 percent during the same years in states where abortion was illegal except in cases of life endangerment. One researcher has estimated that the legalization of abortion, and the subsequent reduction of both unwanted childbirth and illegal abortion, prevented 1,500 pregnancy-related deaths nationwide by 1983.

Because many of the women who have an abortion are at high risk of a poor pregnancy outcome, legal abortion has also been associated with a reduction in the proportion of infants born at low birth weight and a decrease in the neonatal mortality rate (the number of infants who die during their first month per 1,000 live births). The availability of legal abortion was the single most important factor in the significant decrease in neonatal mortality between 1964 and 1977. Abortion alone was responsible for a reduction of 1.5 neonatal deaths per 1,000 live births among whites and 2.5 per 1,000 live births among blacks. According to an Institute of Medicine study, the data "suggest that the significant increase in the availability of abortion between the late 1960s and the mid-1970s contributed to the gradual deadline in low-birthweight rates over the same period, although the magnitude of the influence has not been well-defined."

Thousands of couples at high risk of bearing children with severe disorders are willing to become pregnant only because they know that prenatal genetic testing and abortion services can help prevent the birth of a seriously impaired child. Further, the number of infants born with Down syndrome in 1976 in the state of Washington would have been 64 percent higher, without legal abortion; 43 percent of the decline in the number of Down syndrome cases in Hawaii between 1963-1969 and 1971-1977 was due to legal abortion.

Since 70 percent of the women having an abortion in 1987 said they intended to have children in the future, any adverse effect on a woman's ability to bear healthy children in the future would be cause for serious concern.

In an attempt to examine these risks, researchers from the Centers for Disease Control and The Population Council conducted an extensive review of the worldwide literature on the effect of abortion on future childbearing ability. After examining studies from 21 countries, including the United States, they concluded that vacuum aspiration does not pose a measurable risk to a woman's future childbearing ability.

Compared with women who carry their first pregnancies to term, women who terminate their first pregnancies by a vacuum aspiration abortion are at no greater risk of subsequent infertility or ectopic pregnancy. A single induced abortion performed by vacuum aspiration—the method used in more than nine out of 10 abortions in the United States today—does not increase the risk of miscarriage, stillbirth, infant mortality or congenital malformations. Further, a woman who has a vacuum aspiration abortion is at no added risk of either having a low-birth-weight infant or suffering major complications during future pregnancies or deliveries.

More Research Needed

The researchers further concluded that studies of the effects of multiple abortions "do not support a firm conclusion about whether the number of induced abortions per se produces any increased risk of adverse outcomes in subsequent . . . pregnancies." While some studies have linked multiple abortions to future difficulty in bearing children, the abortions most frequently implicated were performed using the D&C [dilation and curettage] method, which is rarely used for abortions in the United States today.

In short, while a single abortion does not appear to have any adverse implications for subsequent childbearing, less research has focused on multiple abortions performed using modern surgical procedures or second-trimester abortions. Additional research is necessary to determine whether they have an impact on a woman's future ability to bear healthy children.

"Unfortunately for hundreds of thousands of women, their 'safe and easy' abortions proved to be neither safe nor easy."

Legal Abortion Has Not Improved Women's Health

David C. Reardon

Abortion, like most medical procedures, involves some risk of physical complications for women. In the following viewpoint, David C. Reardon argues that 10 percent of abortions result in infection or hemorrhaging. This percentage, Reardon maintains, does not include unreported complications or women's long-term complications. He also states that abortion is especially risky for the more than one hundred thousand women who have second and third trimester abortions annually. Reardon is the founding director of the Elliot Institute for Social Science Research.

As you read, consider the following questions:

1. In Reardon's opinion, do doctors adequately notify women of the risks of abortion?
2. Why does the author criticize doctors for preferring saline abortions over prostaglandin abortions, which he says are safer?
3. What are some of the long-term physical complications of women who have abortions, according to Reardon?

Excerpted, with permission, from *Aborted Women: Silent No More* by David C. Reardon. Chicago: Loyola University Press, 1987. Copyright © 1987 by David C. Reardon.

Abortion is a surgical procedure in which a woman's body is forcibly entered and her pregnancy is forcibly "terminated." Because it is intrusive, and because it disrupts a natural process (pregnancy), abortion poses both short-term and long-term risks to the health and well-being of the aborted woman. Abortion is never without risks.

A few abortion advocates continue to insist that abortion is so safe as to be virtually "risk free," but such claims are exaggerations resulting from some blind belief in the slogans and clichés fostered by the early abortion reformers. In contrast to these few abortion zealots, most defenders of abortion, particularly those in the health fields, admit that there are inherent risks to abortion. Within the medical profession the intense debate is not over whether there are risks or not but over how often complications will occur. Some claim the risks are "acceptable," while others insist they are not.

Answering the question "How safe is abortion?" is crucial to any public policy on abortion; but it is even more crucial to the women facing the abortion decision. Unfortunately for hundreds of thousands of women, their "safe and easy" abortions proved to be neither safe nor easy. Even more outrageous is the fact that almost none of these women were given a realistic assessment of the risks of abortion. . . .

Complications of Abortion

The rate of complications following a medical procedure is known as the morbidity rate. For the reasons cited above, the morbidity rate due to abortion in America is unknown, though a few hospital studies have been done. But while the rate of complications is uncertain, the variety of complications which occur is well documented.

Over one hundred potential complications have been associated with abortion. Some of these complications can be immediately spotted, such as a puncture of the uterus or other organs, convulsions, or cardiac arrest. Other complications reveal themselves within a few days, such as a slow hemorrhage, pulmonary embolisms, infection and fever. Still other complications are long-term in nature, usually the result of damage to the reproductive system, and may result in chronic infection, an inability to carry a subsequent pregnancy to term, or sterility. These latent complications may not be apparent until a later pregnancy is attempted or until the uterus is so infected as to require removal. Thus, an abortion recorded as complication-free in a short-term study might in fact have caused long-term damage. Thus, as many investigators have discovered, short-term studies of abortion complications reveal only the tip of the iceberg. Indeed, the longer women are kept under surveillance after an abortion, the higher are the reported rates of latent morbidity. Women who may appear physically unaffected by an abortion after a one year follow-up may be found to be severely affected by the abortion as many as ten to fifteen years later.

High Rates of Complication

Because of the large number of possible complications, it is difficult for any medical study to check for them all, especially the more elusive ones. Furthermore, because of the great time variation between short-term complications and long-term complications, no major scientific studies have been done to tabulate both.

After noting all of these qualifications, a few general observations can be made. First, every type of abortion procedure carries significant risks. Second, the earlier the abortion is done, the lower is the rate of immediate and short-term "major" complications. Third, every type of abortion procedure poses a significant long-term threat to a woman's reproductive health. Fourth, the younger the patient, the greater the long-term risks to her reproductive system.

Legal Abortions Are Not Safer

Not only do deaths from illegal abortions continue to occur, but constitutional abortion has added its own casualties to the maternal mortality statistics—in some cases simply bringing "back-alley" practitioners to the clinics. Indeed exhaustive study has shown that maternal deaths resulting from legal abortions are replacing those due to illegal abortions.

Mark E. Chopko, Phillip H. Harris, and Helen M. Alvare, *Phi Kappa Phi Journal*, Fall 1989.

Overall, the rate of immediate and short-term complications is no less than 10 percent. This figure is based on a *reported* 100,000 abortion complications in 1977, when the total number of legal abortions in that year was approximately one million. This 10 percent morbidity rate, it should be remembered, is an undisputed *minimum* rate for immediate and short-term complications. It does not include unreported complications or long-range complications such as infertility. As we will see, the evidence indicates that the actual morbidity rate is probably much higher.

Almost 90 percent of all abortions are performed by suction curettage, commonly known as vacuum abortions. In this procedure, the vagina and cervix are forcibly dilated with progressively larger tapered cylinders called dilators. Dilation provides the abortionist with the necessary "working room" through which he inserts the abortion instruments, in this case a cutting instrument attached to a high-powered vacuum (29 times more powerful than a home vacuum). With this device, the abortionist dismembers the "products of conception" (i.e. the unborn child and its placenta) and simultaneously vacuums out the pieces. Abortionists insist that in skilled hands suction curettage is the safest form of abortion. Many physicians disagree.

According to two independent studies, the immediate or short-term complication rate for vacuum abortions is approximately 12 percent. The reported "major" complication rate (strictly defined to include only life-threatening complications) is 4000 per million. Obviously, defining "major" complications in restrictive terms would make abortion appear safer than it really is. Considering both immediate and long-term complications, a major German study found that the total morbidity rate for vacuum aspiration abortions exceeded 31 percent.

Because the abortionist operates blindly, by sense of feel only, the cutting/suction device is potentially deadly. Perforation of the uterus is one of the most common complications (this can occur during dilation or evacuation) which leads to severe hemorrhage and can occasionally result in damage to other internal organs. In a few recorded cases, abortionists have inadvertently sucked out several feet of intestines in a matter of only a few seconds.

Another common complication results from failure to extract all the "products of conception." If a limb or skull is left in the uterus, or if a portion of the placenta remains intact, severe infection may result, causing severe cramping and bleeding. Treatment may require another dilation followed by mechanical curettage and antibiotics. If the infection becomes too advanced or is persistent, a hysterectomy will be necessary to remove the diseased uterus.

Dangers of Embolisms

Third, as with all forms of abortion, suction curettage results in a high incidence of embolisms. An embolism is an obstruction of a blood vessel by a foreign substance such as air, fat, tissue, or a blood clot. Usually, such a blockage is minor and goes unnoticed and is eventually dissolved. But if the block occurs in the brain or heart, it may result in a stroke or heart attack. If it occurs in the lungs, it may result in a pulmonary thromboembolism. This condition may occur anywhere from two to fifty days after an abortion and is a relatively frequent major complication. In one group of abortion-related deaths, pulmonary embolisms were the second most common cause of death. Because of the nature of embolisms, these abortion fatalities are unpredictable and often unavoidable. This risk, like most others, is seldom revealed to women during counseling at abortion clinics, even though it is widely known in medical circles. Pulmonary embolisms are reported to afflict about 200 aborted women each year.

Miscarriages Likelier After Repeated Abortions

A study of women at the Boston Hospital for Women conducted during 1976-1978 concluded that women who had two or more induced abortions were 2.7 times more likely to have future first trimester spontaneous abortions (miscarriage) and 3.2 times more likely to have a second trimester incomplete abortion than were women with no history of induced abortion.

Association for Interdisciplinary Research in Values Newsletter, Summer 1989.

Fourth, due the the rich blood supply around the uterus during pregnancy, local and general anesthesia during abortions are particularly risky. Anesthesia complications during first trimester abortions are fairly common and unpredictable. When an adverse reaction to anesthetics occurs in an outpatient abortion clinic, there is generally little equipment and expertise available on the site to deal with the emergency. Convulsions, heart arrest, and death are not an uncommon result of these circumstances. In one study of 74 women killed by legal abortions, anesthesia complications ranked as the third leading cause of death. The officially reported rate of anesthesia complications is 20 per 100,000 first trimester abortions.

The nine most common "major" complications resulting from vacuum abortions are: infection, excessive bleeding, embolism, ripping or perforation of the uterus, anesthesia complications, convulsions, hemorrhage, cervical injury, and endotoxic shock. "Minor" complications include: minor infections, bleeding, fevers and chills, second degree burns, chronic abdominal pain, vomiting, gastro-intestinal disturbances, weight loss, painful or disrupted menstrual cycles, and Rh sensitization.

A word about the last item: only 42 percent of aborted women receive Rh screening prior to their abortions; and even for the minority that are tested, the analysis of the blood samples are often rushed and inaccurate. Unless a woman with Rh negative blood receives a RhoGam injection immediately after the abortion, sensitization may result. In a later "wanted pregnancy" this sensitization may endanger both the life of the mother and her child, a complication which could no longer be considered "minor."

Dilation and curettage is very similar to suction curettage but is used primarily in late first trimester and early second trimester abortions. It differs from suction abortions in that instead of vacuuming out the "products of conception," the abortionist manually dismembers the fetus and scrapes the organs out of the uterus and into a basin. Because it uses sharper instruments and involves more scraping, D&C abortions typically result in much greater blood loss and a higher rate of overall complications.

The types of complications associated with D&C abortions are virtually the same as with vacuum abortions, but are approximately 20 percent more frequent.

Saline Abortions

Each year there are between 100,000 and 150,000 second and third trimester abortions. Most of these are saline abortions. The rate of "major" complications associated with saline abortion is reported to be about five times greater than for first trimester suction abortions.

In a saline abortion, also known as a "salting out," a concentrated salt solution is injected into the amniotic sack surrounding the baby. This solution burns the skin of the fetus and slowly poisons his system, resulting in vasodilation, edema, congestion, hemorrhage, shock and death. This process takes from one to three hours, during which the distressed unborn kicks, thrusts, and writhes in its attempts to escape. Twelve to forty-eight hours after the child dies, the mother's hormonal system shifts in recognition of this fact and she goes into natural labor. Normally, within 72 hours after the injection, she will deliver a dead fetus.

The technique of saline abortion was originally developed in the concentration camps of Nazi Germany. In Japan, where abortion has been legalized since the 1940s, the saline abortion technique has been outlawed because it is "extraordinarily dangerous." Indeed, in the United States saline abortion is second only to heart transplants as the elective surgery with the highest fatality rate. Despite this fact, state laws attempting to prohibit saline abortions because of their great risk to aborting women have been declared unconstitutional by the courts.

Severe infections and hemorrhages are extremely common following saline abortions. In addition, seepage of the salt solution into the woman's blood system may result in life-threatening coagulation problems. Incomplete abortions and retained placentas occur in from 40 to 55 percent of all cases, the correction of which requires additional surgery. Furthermore, infections or uterine damage incurred during saline abortions frequently require removal of the uterus.

In a technique similar to saline abortions, the chemical prostaglandin is injected into the amniotic fluid. But instead of killing the unborn outright, this method induces intense contractions of the uterus and causes forced labor. Usually the child dies during the trauma of premature labor, but frequently it does not. This results in one the most disturbing "complications" of prostaglandin abortions, a live birth.

When prostaglandins were first introduced, there was great hope among abortionists that this new technique would be safer than saline injections. But when six women died and a large number of "aborted" babies were delivered *alive*, the enthusiasm for prostaglandins dwindled rapidly.

Frequent complications associated with prostaglandin abortions include spontaneous ruptures in the uterine wall, convulsions, hemorrhage, coagulation defects, and cervical injury. Incomplete abortions are also very common. In these cases the decay of retained tissue may result in severe infections, prolonged hospitalization, additional surgery, and in many cases the need for an emergency hysterectomy.

In sum, rather than replacing saline abortions, prostaglandins have simply caused a debate within the aborting community as to which method is the most dangerous. Oddly enough, however, although the evidence seems to indicate that prostaglandins are slightly less dangerous, most abortionists continue to prefer saline abortions. The reason for this is simple. Live births following prostaglandin abortions are extremely disturbing to both the medical staff and the mothers. In other words, a higher priority is being placed on killing the fetus than on providing the safest way for a woman to be rid of the pregnancy. . . .

Abortion's Dismal Record

This viewpoint has dealt with the subject of physical complications related to abortion. The subject is complex because so little is known. The reporting of abortion complications is not required by law and there are numerous motives for not reporting them. All evidence seems to confirm that *underreporting is the rule rather than the exception.*

But even assuming that all complications and deaths from legal abortion are reported, the safety record of abortion is dismal. The *reported* rate of immediate complications following induced abortion is fully 10 percent. The frequency of late complications is not documented in American statistics, but based on foreign experience, long-term complications can be expected in from 17 to 50 percent of all aborted women. Most of these long-term complications result in partial or total infertility, and an increased risk of ectopic pregnancies, miscarriages, and premature births. These risks are especially high among young women who have not yet had their families.

The evidence overwhelmingly proves that the morbidity and

200

mortality rates of legal abortion are several times higher than that for carrying a pregnancy to term. But this fact has been largely suppressed in America for political and population control reasons.

All of these points, of course, are open to dispute to the degree that it is impossible to prove the cause of any health problem. Just as tobacco growers and cigarette companies continue to claim that the "causal link" between smoking and lung cancer has not yet been "proven," so do abortion providers insist that the dangers of abortion are still "uncertain."

But one thing is certain. Despite the legalization of abortion, complications and deaths continue to occur, and little or nothing is being done to warn women about the possibility of such negative results. No one doubts that legal abortion is marginally safer than illegal abortion, but neither is there any doubt that decriminalization has encouraged more women to undergo abortions than ever before. Risk goes down, but numbers go up. This combination means that though the odds of any particular woman suffering ill effects from an abortion have dropped, the *total* number of women who suffer and die from abortion is far greater than ever before.

Evaluating Sources of Information

When historians study and interpret past events, they use two kinds of sources: primary and secondary. Primary sources are eyewitness accounts. For example, a book written by a prominent abortion rights activist who argues that abortion should always be legal would be a primary source. A magazine article describing the book would be a secondary source. Primary and secondary sources may be decades or even hundreds of years old, and often historians find that the sources offer conflicting and contradictory information. To fully evaluate documents and assess their accuracy, historians analyze the credibility of the documents' authors and, in the case of secondary sources, analyze the credibility of the information the authors used.

Historians are not the only people who encounter conflicting information, however. Anyone who reads a daily newspaper, watches television, or just talks to different people will encounter many different views. Writers and speakers use sources of information to support their own statements. Thus, critical thinkers, just like historians, must question the writer's or speaker's sources of information as well as the writer or speaker.

While there are many criteria that can be applied to assess the accuracy of a primary or secondary source, for this activity you will be asked to apply three. For each source listed on the following page, ask yourself the following questions: First, did the person actually see or participate in the event he or she is reporting? This will help you determine the credibility of the information—an eyewitness to an event is an extremely valuable source. Second, does the person have a vested interest in the report? Assessing the person's social status, professional affiliations, nationality, and religious or political beliefs will be helpful in considering this question. By evaluating this you will be able to determine how objective the person's report may be. Third, how qualified is the author to be making the statements he or she is making? Consider what the person's profession is and how he or she might know about the event. Someone who has spent years being involved with or studying the issue may be able to offer more information than someone who simply is offering an uneducated opinion; for example, a politician or layperson.

Keeping the above criteria in mind, imagine you are writing a paper on the abortion issue. You decide to cite an equal number of primary and secondary sources. Listed below are several sources that may be useful for your research. *Place a P next to those descriptions you believe are primary sources. Place an S next to those descriptions you believe are secondary sources.* Next, based on the above criteria, *rank the primary sources, assigning the number (1) to what appears to be the most valuable, (2) to the source likely to be the second-most valuable, and so on, until all the primary sources are ranked. Then rank the secondary sources, again using the above criteria.*

P or S

Rank in
Importance

———— 1. A report from the Centers for Disease Control listing the annual number of U.S. abortions. ————

———— 2. A magazine article written by a woman who describes the traumatic experience of her abortion. ————

———— 3. A National Organization for Women pamphlet outlining a university study on the safety of abortion. ————

———— 4. A book written by a doctor who refuses to perform any more abortions. ————

———— 5. A televised debate between the presidents of the National Right to Life Committee and Planned Parenthood Federation. ————

———— 6. A *New York Times* report of a demonstration against abortion. ————

———— 7. A magazine review of Laurence Tribe's book on abortion, *Clash of the Absolutes.* ————

———— 8. A *Newsweek* magazine article describing the U.S. Supreme Court's decision in the *Roe v. Wade* case. ————

———— 9. A television interview with abortion rights advocate Gloria Steinem. ————

———— 10. An article written by a *Wall Street Journal* reporter covering the Louisiana state legislature's passage of a restrictive abortion bill. ————

Periodical Bibliography

The following articles have been selected to supplement the diverse views presented in this chapter.

Nancy Amidei — "Variant Views on Abortion," *Commonweal*, October 26, 1990.

Fred Barnes — "Abortive Issue," *The New Republic*, December 4, 1989.

Christianity Today — "Voters Send Mixed Signals on Abortion," December 17, 1990.

Eleanor Clift — "Taking Issue with NOW," *Newsweek*, August 14, 1989.

Ted Gest — 'The Abortion Furor," *U.S. News & World Report*, July 17, 1989.

Kathryn Kolbert and Julie Mertus — "Pro-choice: Keeping the Pressure On," *Ms.*, January/February 1991.

Morton Kondracke — "The New Abortion Wars," *The New Republic*, August 28, 1989.

David Kupelian and Mark Masters — "Pro-choice 1990: Skeletons in the Closet," *New Dimensions*, October 1990. Available from New Dimensions, 874 NE 7th St., Grants Pass, OR 97526.

Richard Lacayo — "The Shifting Politics of Abortion," *Time*, October 23, 1989.

J. Ralph Lindgren — "Protecting Reproductive Freedom in a Conservative Era," *USA Today*, January 1991.

Margaret Liu McConnell — "Living with Roe v. Wade," *Commentary*, November 1990.

Kate Michelman — "The Central Question Is, Who Decides?" *The World & I*, October 1989.

Richard J. Neuhaus — "After Roe," *National Review*, December 31, 1989.

Newsweek — "The Future of Abortion," July 17, 1989.

Rosalind P. Petchesky — "Giving Women a Real Choice," *The Nation*, May 28, 1990.

Gloria Steinem — "A Basic Human Right," *Ms.*, July/August 1989.

William H. Willimon — "A Uniquely Christian Stand on Abortion," *The Christian Century*, February 27, 1991.

Organizations to Contact

The editors have compiled the following list of organizations that are concerned with the issues debated in this book. All of them have publications or information available for interested readers. The descriptions are derived from materials provided by the organizations. This list was compiled upon the date of publication. Names and phone numbers of organizations are subject to change.

American Civil Liberties Union (ACLU)
132 W. 43rd St.
New York, NY 10036
(212) 944-9800

The ACLU champions the rights set forth in the Declaration of Independence and the Constitution. Among many civil rights issues, the ACLU works for safe and legal abortions for all women and opposes parental consent abortion laws. The ACLU publishes the monthly newsletter *First Principles,* the bimonthly newspaper *Civil Liberties,* and the booklet *Shattering the Dreams of Young Women: The Tragic Consequences of Parental Involvement Laws.*

American Life League (ALL)
PO Box 1350
Stafford, VA 22554
(703) 659-4171

ALL promotes family values and opposes abortion. It provides educational materials, books, flyers, and programs for local, state, and national pro-family organizations that oppose abortion. Publications include a weekly newsletter, the monthly newsletter *All About Issues,* the booklet *Exceptions: Abandoning "The Least of These My Brethren,"* and a pamphlet, *Rape and Incest Exceptions to Abortion Law: Why They Are Bad Policy.*

Americans United for Life (AUL)
343 S. Dearborn St., Suite 1804
Chicago, IL 60604
(312) 786-9494

AUL promotes legislation to make abortion illegal. The organization operates a library and a legal-resource center. It publishes the quarterly newsletter *Lex Vitae,* the monthly newsletter *AUL Insights,* and booklets, including *The Beginning of Human Life* and *The Limits of the Law: Reflections on the Abortion Debate.*

Catholics for a Free Choice (CFFC)
1436 U St. NW, Suite 301
Washington, DC 20009
(202) 638-1706

CFFC supports the right to legal abortion and promotes family planning to reduce the incidence of abortion and to increase women's choice in childbearing and child rearing. It publishes the bimonthly newsletter *Conscience,* the booklet *The History of Abortion in the Catholic Church,* and the brochure *You Are Not Alone.*

Center for Population Options (CPO)
1012 14th St. NW, Suite 1200
Washington, DC 20005
(202) 347-5700

The CPO is an educational organization dedicated to improving the quality of life for adolescents by reducing the incidence of unwanted teenage pregnancies and advocating minors' access to legal abortion. Publications include the book *Teen Pregnancy and Too-Early Childbearing: Public Costs, Personal Consequences,* the fact book *Adolescents and Abortion: Choice in Crisis,* and the guide *Adolescent Abortion and Parental Involvement Laws.*

Christian Action Council (CAC)
101 W. Broad St., Suite 500
Falls Church, VA 22046
(703) 237-2100

The council, which opposes abortion, is committed to reversing the U.S. Supreme Court's decision legalizing abortion. It seeks to persuade Christians to become active in the political discussion of abortion issues. Publications include the quarterly bulletin *Action Line.*

Eagle Forum
PO Box 618
Alton, IL 62002
(618) 462-5415

The forum, founded by Phyllis Schlafly, promotes education and traditional family values. It opposes abortion and abortion rights. Publications include the monthly *Phyllis Schlafly Report.*

Feminists for Life of America
811 E. 47th St.
Kansas City, MO 64110
(816) 753-2130

This organization is comprised of individuals united to secure the right to life, from conception to natural death, for all human beings. It believes that legal abortion exploits women. The group supports a Human Life Amendment, the Equal Rights Amendment, and other methods it believes will achieve respect for life and equality. Publications include the quarterly *Sisterlife,* the book *Prolife Feminism: Different Voices,* the booklet *Early Feminist Case Against Abortion,* and the pamphlet *Abortion Does Not Liberate Women.*

Alan Guttmacher Institute
111 Fifth Ave.
New York, NY 10003
(212) 254-5656

The institute is an abortion research group that advocates the right to safe and legal abortion. It provides extensive statistical information on abortion and voluntary population control. Publications include the bimonthly *Family Planning Perspectives* magazine, the booklet *Abortion and Women's Health: A Turning Point in America,* and the fact sheets *Abortion in the U.S.* and *Teenage Sexual and Reproductive Behavior in the U.S.*

Human Life Center
University of Steubenville
Steubenville, OH 43952
(614) 282-9953

The center, which opposes abortion, promotes Roman Catholic teaching concerning the sanctity of life. It publishes a pamphlet series for teens and two quarterlies, *Human Life Issues* and *International Review of Natural Family Planning.*

Human Life Foundation (HLF)
150 E. 35th St.
New York, NY 10016
(212) 685-5210

The foundation opposes abortion and serves as a charitable and educational support group for individuals concerned about abortion, euthanasia, and infanticide. It offers financial support to organizations that provide women with alternatives to abortion. Publications include the quarterly *Human Life Review* and books and pamphlets on abortion.

National Abortion Federation (NAF)
1436 U St. NW, Suite 103
Washington, DC 20009
(202) 667-5881

The federation is committed to making safe, legal abortions accessible to all women. It provides information to hospitals, clinics, feminist health centers, and other groups that offer abortion services. It also instructs women on how to choose an abortion facility. Publications include the booklets *Unsure About Your Pregnancy?* and *Celebrating Roe v. Wade: Dramatic Improvements in Public Health,* the bulletin *Legal Abortion Is Safe Abortion,* and fact sheets.

National Abortion Rights Action League (NARAL)
1101 14th St. NW
Washington, DC 20005
(202) 408-4600

NARAL is one of the largest membership and lobbying organizations working solely to keep abortion a safe, legal, and available option for all women. The league works with legislatures, the public, and students to promote its stance on abortion. It publishes the quarterly newsletter *NARAL News.*

National Conference of Catholic Bishops (NCCB)
3211 Fourth St. NE
Washington, DC 20017-1194
(202) 541-3000

The NCCB, which opposes abortion, is an institution of U.S. Roman Catholic bishops. It suggests that states restrict abortion by passing parental consent laws and strict licensing laws for facilities that perform abortions. The conference publishes the annual magazine *Respect Life* and the monthly newsletter *Life Insight.*

National Organization for Women (NOW)
1000 16th St. NW, Suite 700
Washington, DC 20004
(202) 331-0066

NOW, the largest women's rights group in the United States, supports safe and legal abortions and birth control. It is involved in political action and in educating the public on women's issues, including abortion. The organization's magazine, *NOW Times,* is published three times each year.

National Right to Life Committee (NRLC)
419 Seventh St. NW, Suite 500
Washington, DC 20004
(202) 626-8800

The committee is one of the largest organizations that oppose abortion. It encourages ratification of a constitutional amendment to protect all human life. The NRLC supports abortion alternatives such as adoption. Publications include the biweekly *National Right to Life News* and the pamphlet *Challenge to Be Pro-Life.*

Planned Parenthood Federation of America (PPFA)
810 Seventh Ave.
New York, NY 10019
(212) 541-7800

Planned Parenthood is a national organization that promotes family planning. Through its numerous clinics, PPFA provides contraception, abortion, and sterilization services. It publishes a number of pamphlets such as *Abortions: Questions and Answers, Five Ways to Prevent Abortion,* and *Nine Reasons Why Abortions Are Legal.*

Pro-Life Action League
6160 N. Cicero, Suite 210
Chicago, IL 60646
(312) 777-2900

The league advocates the prohibition of abortion through a constitutional amendment. It lobbies for legislation limiting abortion and also conducts protests at abortion clinics. The league publishes bulletins and brochures, along with the monthly *Action News* and the book *Closed: Ninety-nine Ways to Stop Abortion.*

Sex Information and Educational Council of the U.S. (SIECUS)
32 Washington Place
New York, NY 10003
(212) 673-3850

SIECUS is a group that advocates abortion rights. It is one of the nation's largest clearinghouses for sex information and it reviews books on human sexuality and compiles annotated bibliographies of sex-education resources. SIECUS publishes the *SIECUS Report* newsletter and books, including *Oh No! What Do I Do Now?*

Women Exploited by Abortion (WEBA)
Route 1, PO Box 821
Venus, TX 76084
(214) 366-3600

WEBA is an organization of women who have had abortions but now oppose them. It offers emotional support to women who regret having had abortions and counsels women considering abortion. WEBA publishes the pamphlets *Before You Make the Decision, Joy Comes in the Mourning,* and *Surviving Abortion.*

Bibliography of Books

Kathryn Payne Addelson — *Impure Thoughts: Essays on Philosophy, Feminism and Ethics.* Philadelphia: Temple University Press, 1991.

John Ankerberg and John Weldon — *When Does Life Begin?* Brentwood, TN: Wolgemuth & Hyatt, 1989.

Ninia Baehr — *Abortion Without Apology: Radical History for the 1990s.* Boston: South End Press, 1990.

Robert M. Baird and Stuart E. Rosenbaum, eds. — *The Ethics of Abortion: Pro-Life vs. Pro-Choice.* Buffalo: Prometheus Books, 1989.

Mark Belz — *Suffer the Little Children: Christians, Abortion, and Civil Disobedience.* Westchester, IL: Crossway Books, 1989.

Angela Bonavoglia, ed. — *The Choices We Made: Twenty-five Women and Men Speak Out About Abortion.* New York: Random House, 1991.

Judie Brown and Brian Young — *Exceptions: Abandoning "The Least of These My Brethren."* Stafford, VA: American Life League, 1990.

Celeste M. Condit — *Decoding Abortion Rhetoric: Communicating Social Change.* Urbana: University of Illinois Press, 1990.

Henry P. David et al., eds. — *Born Unwanted: Developmental Effects of Denied Abortion.* New York: Springer Publishing, 1988.

Susan E. Davis, ed. — *Women Under Attack: Backlash and the Fight for Reproductive Freedom.* Boston: South End Press, 1988.

Edd Doerr and James W. Prescott — *Abortion Rights and Fetal "Personhood."* Long Beach, CA: Centerline Press, 1989.

Diane E. Fitzpatrick — *The History of Abortion in the United States: A Working Bibliography of Journal Articles.* Monticello, IL: Vance Bibliographies, 1991.

Paul Fowler — *Abortion: Toward an Evangelical Consensus.* Portland, OR: Multnomah Press, 1987.

Marlene Gerber Fried — *From Abortion to Reproductive Freedom.* Boston: South End Press, 1990.

Maggie Gallagher — *Enemies of Eros.* Chicago: Bonus Books, 1989.

Ian J. Gentles — *A Time to Choose Life: Women, Abortion, and Human Rights.* Toronto: Stoddart, 1990.

Faye D. Ginsburg — *Contested Lives: The Abortion Debate in an American Community.* Berkeley: University of California Press, 1989.

Mary Ann Glendon — *Abortion and Divorce in Western Law.* Cambridge, MA: Harvard University Press, 1987.

Thomas A. Glessner — *Achieving an Abortion-Free America by 2001.* Portland, OR: Multnomah Press, 1990.

Rachel Benson Gold — *Abortion and Women's Health: A Turning Point for America?* New York: Alan Guttmacher Institute, 1990.

Michael F. Goodman — *What Is A Person?* Clifton, NJ: Humana Press, 1988.

Linda Gordon — *Woman's Body, Woman's Right: A Social History of Birth Control in America.* rev. ed. New York: Penguin USA, 1990.

George Grant	*Grand Illusions—The Legacy of Planned Parenthood.* Brentwood, TN: Wolgemuth & Hyatt, 1988.
Clifford Grobstein	*Science and the Unborn.* New York: Basic Books, 1988.
Betsy Hartmann	*Reproductive Rights and Wrongs.* New York: Harper & Row, 1987.
Stanley K. Henshaw	*Teenage Pregnancy in the United States.* New York: Alan Guttmacher Institute, 1989.
Rosalind Hursthouse	*Beginning Lives.* Oxford, England: Basil Blackwell, 1987.
Patricia Beattie Jung and Thomas A. Shannon	*Abortion and Catholicism: The American Debate.* New York: Crossroad Publishing, 1988.
Thomas G. Klasen	*A Pro-Life Manifesto.* Westchester, IL: Crossway Books, 1988.
James W. Knight and Joan C. Callahan	*Preventing Birth: Contemporary Methods and Related Moral Controversies.* Salt Lake City: University of Utah Press, 1989.
J. Gordon Melton	*The Churches Speak On—Abortion: Official Statements from Religious Bodies and Ecumenical Organizations.* Detroit: Gale Research, 1989.
Ellen Messer and Kathryn E. May	*Back Rooms: Voices from the Abortion Era.* New York: Simon & Schuster, 1988.
Sue Nathanson	*Soul Murder.* New York: New American Library Books, 1989.
National Abortion Rights Action League	*The Voices of Women: Abortion, in Their Own Words.* Washington, DC: NARAL, 1989.
Susan and Marvin Olasky	*More than Kindness: A Compassionate Approach to Crisis Childbearing.* Westchester, IL: Crossway Books, 1990.
Rosalind P. Petchesky	*Abortion and Women's Choice: The State, Sexuality, and Reproductive Freedom.* rev. ed. Boston: Northeastern University Press, 1990.
Anne Pierson and Carol Risser	*Fifty-two Simple Things You Can Do to Be Pro-Life.* Minneapolis: Bethany House, 1991.
Janet Podell, ed.	*Abortion.* New York: H.W. Wilson, 1990.
Shirley L. Radl	*Over Our Live Bodies: Preserving Choice in America.* Dallas: Steve Davis Publishing, 1989.
David C. Reardon	*Aborted Women: Silent No More.* Chicago: Loyola University Press, 1987.
Charles E. Rice	*No Exception: A Pro-Life Imperative.* Notre Dame, IN: Tyholland Press, 1990.
Hyman Rodman, Betty Sarvis, and Joy Walker Bonar	*The Abortion Question.* New York: Columbia University Press, 1987.
Robert Ruff	*Aborting Planned Parenthood.* Houston: New Vision Press, 1988.
Paul Sachdev, ed.	*International Handbook on Abortion.* New York: Greenwood Press, 1988.
Stephen D. Schwarz	*The Moral Question of Abortion.* Chicago: Loyola University Press, 1990.

Irving J. Sloan	*The Law Governing Abortion, Contraception and Sterilization.* New York: Oceana Publications, 1988.
F. LaGard Smith	*When Choice Becomes God.* Eugene, OR: Harvest House, 1990.
Patricia Spallone	*Beyond Conception: The New Politics of Reproduction.* Granby, MA: Bergin & Garvey, 1989.
R.C. Sproul	*Abortion: A Rational Look at an Emotional Issue.* Colorado Springs: NavPress, 1990.
Charles Swindoll	*Sanctity of Life: The Inescapable Issue.* Irving, TX: Word Inc., 1990.
Nadine Taub and Sherill Cohen	*Reproductive Laws for the 1990s.* Clifton, NJ: Humana Press, 1989.
Susan N. Terkel	*Abortion: Facing the Issues.* New York: Greenwood Press, 1988.
Phyllis Tickle, ed.	*Confessing Conscience: Churched Women on Abortion.* Nashville: Abingdon Press, 1990.
Sarah L. Tietze and Richard Lincoln, eds.	*Fertility Regulation and the Public Health.* New York: Springer-Verlag, 1987.
Laurence H. Tribe	*Abortion: The Clash of Absolutes.* New York: W.W. Norton, 1990.
Philip Turner, ed.	Men and Women: Sexual Ethics in Turbulent Times. Cambridge, MA: Cowley Publications, 1989.
Judith Welt	*Abortion, Choice, and Contemporary Fiction: The Armageddon of the Maternal Instinct.* Chicago: University of Chicago Press, 1990.
K.B. Welton	*Abortion Is Not a Sin.* Costa Mesa, CA: Pandit Press, 1987.
Denise Winn	*Experiences of Abortion.* London: Macdonald & Co., 1988.

Index